Third Generation Railwayman

In 1857 John Barford's grandfather's brother started work on the Midland Railway. When John joined the LMS at Wellingborough depot in 1932 he was following a family tradition. His grandfather had been an engine driver and his father was still employed as a boilersmith.

In this book he tells of his life as an apprentice fitter, his progression to membership of the breakdown team and finally, the giant leap into the unknown world of management. His dedication, loyalty and obvious love for his chosen career shine through the pages and his story is a valuable record of ways of working now lost and the changes brought by modernisation.

Third Generation Railwayman

by John Barford

APPLE TREE BOOKS

This book may be ordered from bookshops or from
Apple Tree Books, Churchfields, Stonesfield, Witney, Oxfordshire OX29 8PP
01993 891204

e-mail: appletree@cleaver.eclipse.co.uk
Credit card orders should be phoned to 01993 891204

First published in 2011 by
Apple Tree Books
Churchfields, Stonesfield, Witney,
Oxfordshire OX29 8PP

ISBN 978 0 9568589 0 0

The right of John Barford to be identified as author of this work has been asserted in
accordance with the Copyright, Designs and Patents Act 1988

Printed in England by PrintFlow Ltd, London EC1V 7JD.

Contents

Dedication

This book is dedicated to my late wife Kath who, for the 67 years of our married life, was at my side. Kath supported me without complaint during all those times I was away from home, on shiftwork, breakdowns, training courses and relieving at other depots for months on end. She looked after our daughter Rosemary without whom this book would never have been published, and my thanks go to her for all the hours spent turning my notes into a readable account.

Preface

It was Sunday morning. I stood in Wellingborough railway depot next to my Dad, and in my hand I held a cup of tea poured for me from a real billycan. I listened with half an ear as Dad chatted with his workmates who were on duty. The rest of my attention was fixed on the sights, the sounds, the smells all around me. The depot was quieter on Sundays but beyond the voices I could hear other noises - the hiss of steam, a hammer on metal, a shout of laughter and the distant clatter of engines shunting.

I knew that soon, my father would lift me up onto a loco and show me how everything worked. Then I could imagine what it would be like to be on the footplate when the power of steam began to push this enormous machine along the rails.

He would show me all round the engine sheds and the machine shop, and I would see the three-foot deep pits where the fitters worked under the engines, and, in the centre of each shed, the 60 foot turntable which was one of the biggest things in the world to me.

I wanted to see the breakdown crane, the coaling plant and the ash pits; most of all the huge Garratt locos which were so big they had to be left outside.

But for now I had to be patient. I was very small and the men in their grease-marked overalls towered above me. I could smell oil and engine smoke and I held on to my cup of tea tightly. I knew I would see it all soon, but for the moment I was happy to be standing with this group. I did not belong yet but I knew that I wanted to be like these workmen and be a part of this one day.

Yes, this would be my life, as it had been my father's and his father's.

1 A child at the depot

I had to be careful at school. My twin sister, Roma, and I walked up to Victoria Elementary School every day from our house near the railway lines and the allotment plots and not too far from the station.

My problem was that I was a small lad; in fact I was probably the smallest person in the school. This remained the case until I left to go to work so there was always a bit of a wariness and tension in my schooldays. If everyone is bigger than you, you have to watch your back a great deal. You have to be careful what you say and do – and you can forget all about making jokes at anyone else's expense.

But in the 1920s school was not often something that children enjoyed. If a pupil misbehaved or failed at lessons, teachers used harsh methods of punishment. I couldn't write an essay. ('Composition', we called it.) I remember we were given half an hour to write about 'An Umbrella' one day. I struggled badly with this and at the end of the lesson had only written two lines. I knew what was coming and held out my hand for four strokes of the cane. It hurt. The blows left terrible blue ridges on a boy's fingers, and the only way to ease the pain was to hold on to the cold steel frame of the desk.

Mental arithmetic was a different story. I could do this and I rather liked it. Art was also a favourite lesson and it was in this that I had my one and only school success. We had to paint a picture of an autumn leaf. This was going quite well until I smeared it with my hand and smudged my carefully painted colours together. I was disappointed and was very surprised when my teacher liked the effect so much that she declared my painting "the best in class".

School was hard and without much variation but once we went on a very special outing to Southampton. We all got on the train at Wellingborough station and travelled down to the docks to see the *RMS Mauritania*. Built in 1906, at almost 32,000 tons she was the largest ship in the world and held the Blue Riband (for the fastest transatlantic crossing) for 22 years.

I have no idea how it came to be arranged that a party of over-excited schoolchildren from Northamptonshire would be allowed to board this vast liner in which sailed the rich and famous, but board her we did on that never-

---

Six years old and a railwayman in the making! My father made this wooden engine in 1924.

to-be-forgotten day. No doubt we gazed at the wood panelling, the marble and the tapestries as we went from room to room, but it was the doorways that impressed me most. In each entrance was a raised threshold that we had to step over – a bit like an obstacle race I thought, especially if people were in a hurry. But I supposed it might stop them getting wet if the sea came in during a storm.

Any diversion is welcome to a gang of boys reluctant to get to school. One day we could hardly believe our eyes when, just up ahead, was a cow. It was in a road with no farmyard, and streets away from the cattle market, so it was a very odd thing to see. But where it had come from did not concern us. Here was a big cow running wild in the street. What luck! This was something we had to see. About ten of us stood in a group and watched while men rushed hither and thither until, eventually, the frightened animal was caught. After it had been tied to a lamppost and things had calmed down, we hurried on to school. Unfortunately we were late now. There was nothing for it but to line up in the hall and wait while the Headmaster fetched the cane. It had almost been worth it.

The river Nene runs through Wellingborough and we boys always made the most of it. We took a drink and bread and cheese with us and spent our time fishing, swimming or just mucking about. But during February or March of 1928 the river froze hard. This was the best thing that could have happened that winter. The surface was solid enough to support people and we rushed down there as soon as we could. We tore about on the ice, falling over and laughing, skidding around and making long slides. We watched as people wearing proper skates glided past.

This went on for some days until the river decided it had had enough of us. There were about 30 people of all ages enjoying themselves on the ice when a loud bang stopped us in our tracks. At the same time chips and splinters of ice flew six feet into the air as a huge crack appeared, about 100 yards long and two yards away from the river bank. For a second or two the world stood still. No-one dared to breathe. Then suddenly everyone began to move, silently, swiftly, and treading as lightly as they could. Within two minutes there was not a soul on the ice. We did feel we had had a lucky escape because the river was quite deep at that point.

So we had plenty of fun and games, but what I really looked forward to were my visits to the railway depot with Dad. He used to take me there on Sunday mornings because there were no bosses about to interfere with us. It meant we could wander round at our leisure and enjoy a cup of tea with the men on duty. There was no stopping for tea during the week.

There were two large sheds, each with a central turntable and capable of housing 24 locomotives. This meant that there were 24 'stabling roads'. This was the name for the rails on which the locos stood awaiting attention, each rail radiating out from the turntable. Dad told me that one shed was used for heavy repairs and examinations; the other for lighter running repairs. He would take me on to one of the locos and explain how things worked; like the regulator for starting, the brake and the reversing lever. He showed me the firebox and I looked through the oval hole at all the tubes and stays. My father was a boilersmith and I knew he had to work inside these fireboxes. I looked at the rather small hole and I looked at him. I simply could not imagine how his six foot, 14 stone frame could pass through. Later on, and still small when I started work, I climbed into a firebox and found it quite claustrophobic, looking back out of such a little hole.

Everything looked so big and heavy to me. I could hardly lift some of the spanners and crowbars used by the fitters and I wondered how on earth they managed to use them. One day we saw a pair of engine wheels which had been taken out of a 2-2-0 Compound locomotive. With a diameter of 7'6", they were the largest wheels made and stood taller than any of the workmen. How could they possibly get them to move?

The biggest locomotives were the Garratts. Wellingborough depot had 14 Garratt 2-6-6-2 locos. These were so big that they could not be housed in the sheds and had to sit in the sidings outside. The numbers refer to the wheels, so a loco described as 2-6-6-2 had two pairs of bogie wheels and two lots of six driving wheels.

When we had finished with the Garratts we made our way to the ash pits. The ashes from a locomotive's fire fall down from the firebox into the ash pan and we used to watch as the men raked out the red hot ashes and threw them into the pits. Once the ashes had cooled, they could be loaded onto wagons and taken away. After this we strolled over to the coaling plant. This machine could lift wagons full of coal weighing 12 tons. Once up high, it would tip the coal out into a hopper, filling the air with noise and dust. Sometimes an engine came along while we were there and was driven to a point under the hopper so that the tender could be filled with coal.

I liked to see the breakdown crane. I knew this had a very important part to play in the smooth running of the railway. If a train came off the rails, the breakdown crew would take this crane out straight away so an engine and any coaches could be re-railed as quickly as possible. The crane could lift 36 tons and attached to it were two coaches. One took the tools and also had a wagon of wooden packing material; the other was used for staff accommodation.

Dad's postcard of the Sharnbrook accident, 1909.

Years ago, a picture postcard was sometimes produced to record an event. Dad used to show me one of these entitled *Accident at Sharnbrook, Bedfordshire. 1909, 04.00 Feb. 4th*. This was an accident of the more serious kind and would have been a very difficult job for a breakdown crew.

On its way to London and travelling at 60mph, the 10.05pm Manchester Express Goods crashed into another goods train standing in Sharnbrook station. The driver, one Arthur Cooper, and fireman, William Hawley, of the express were buried in the wreckage, their bodies being recovered some 13 hours later. The guard, a William Henson, was described as 'severely shaken'. The driver and fireman of the stationary train had heard the express approaching, jumped for it, and were unhurt. Their engine, from Birmingham, was no. 3698, probably a Class 3 FRT (freight) 0-6-0 locomotive. The engine of the express train was no. 385 which could have been a 2-2-0 Class 2 passenger loco; quite speedy but only really capable of taking a small load.

Sometimes beforehand, or sometimes after our tour of the depot, we would join Dad's mates who usually managed to squeeze another two cups of tea out of the billycan. As time went on I began to feel a sense of rightness when I stood there in the group. With my family history it was only natural that railways would get into my blood too, and it was going to be difficult to wait until I left school and, hopefully, started my working life here.

2 Starting work on the LMS Railway

There had been Barfords on the railway since my grandfather's brother William, born in 1857, worked as an engine driver in Northampton. He was a few years older than my grandfather who followed in his footsteps in 1878 and became a driver at Wellingborough. When Dad started work it was as a boilersmith at Wellingborough, beginning in 1914. So with a family like this, was it any wonder that I would feel railways were my destiny too?

The only problem was, when I left Victoria School in 1932, raring to join this illustrious dynasty, there were no vacancies at Wellingborough depot. I knew there had to be an opening for me sooner or later but meanwhile, with no qualifications other than my fairly reasonable aptitude for mental arithmetic and drawing, what was I going to do to fill the time?

I needed to earn some money so I didn't mess about. Quite soon I got a job as an errand boy for a fruit and flower shop with a big nursery attached. My wooden delivery trolley was a really solid piece of work, reinforced with metal and supported on four hefty wheels. At 14 years old I was still pretty small, 4'11" in my socks, and I dare say that at 5st 10lbs there probably wasn't much weight lost between me and that trolley. This was not going to be easy.

The flower shop stood at the bottom of the hill in Sheep Street. My problem was that the people who could afford to buy flowers and spend money on their gardens lived in the Park Road area. There was a gradient of about one in ten for half a mile from the shop up to Park Road. When the trolley was empty it was just manageable, but pushing it up that hill when it was loaded with sacks of loam and peat, or tubs of flowers, took all the strength I had. By the time I had delivered the entire load I was exhausted and, although I tried to run all the way back down the hill, I knew I would be in for a ticking-off for taking too long.

I sometimes felt I was still in school because the manageress had been a teacher and she gave me a piece of her mind after almost every trip. She used to watch me closely with the look I remembered well from the classroom, and it was "Do this, do that…" all day long. But if I bided my time and was very careful, I could sometimes hide a nice juicy apple inside my coat. Eating this on the way home made me feel a lot better. After a day with her, I reckoned I deserved it.

Thankfully, I had only worked at the shop for three months when my chance to go on the railway came up. An apprentice was needed and an interview had been arranged for me with the Motive Power Superintendent. Some 400 staff were employed at Wellingborough depot, about 300 of whom were drivers and firemen. The rest were office workers, foremen, fitters and mates, tubers, boilersmiths and shed staff such as coal and ash plant attendants, boilerwashers, steamraisers and shed sweepers. There was also a blacksmith, coppersmith and a carpenter. Of all these, I most wanted to join the fitters.

And here was my chance. The vacancy was for a seven-year apprenticeship after which I would qualify as a Fitter. On the day of the interview I arrived at the depot in a state of excited anticipation. The superintendent didn't quiz me for too long; he asked me a few questions to make sure I was railway material and then passed me over to the Chief Clerk. Among other things this man told me to take off my shoes and stand up straight in my stockinged feet so that he could measure my height. The rules stated that all applicants should be at least five feet tall, so I knew this could be a problem. My career depended on it – I stretched my neck up and stood as tall as I could. But try as I might, I could not quite reach the target. Luckily for me though, the Chief Clerk got on very well with my father, so, after checking the tape measure, he said, "Go on boy – put your shoes on and you'll make it."

The first hurdles were behind me but before I could be accepted as an employee I had to go to Derby for a medical examination. This went well. The doctor gave me a quick look over, seemed to think I was all there and said, "Right, go on back then, you'll soon grow."

Waiting on Derby platform afterwards, I felt pretty pleased with myself. Not only had I passed the medical, but also, this was the first time I had travelled such a long way on a train by myself. It called for a celebration and I decided to buy a bottle of pop to go with my sandwich. I had sixpence with me, which was two weeks' pocket money, and my mouth must have fallen open when the lady at the counter said, "That'll be fourpence please." I can tell you, I drank that lemonade as though it was champagne.

But it suited my mood – I had passed the last test and I was on the way. Giving in my notice at the flower shop was a genuine pleasure.

I started work at Wellingborough on 2nd August 1932 as an apprentice fitter, on a wage of 9/5d (47p) a week. On that first morning I was sent along to the foreman's office with all the other fitting staff. Outside the office was a tall desk with a sloping top, used by the men when making out repair cards,

With my father before we left for the depot on my first day at work, 2nd August, 1932.

time sheets and so on. At this time of day, most people seemed to use it to lean on whilst waiting for their job allocations. They looked very much at ease to me, laughing and chatting and waiting.

Naturally I wanted to be one of the gang from Day One, so I joined in, leaning my elbow on the lowest part. But of course it was too high for me. I tried very hard to give the right impression, but it's hard to look casual and relaxed with your elbow pressed up against your ear.

For the first year I was placed with an elderly fitter who was approaching retirement. He had been given the job of carrying out examinations every three to five weeks, which involved changing gauge glasses and examining sanders. He was a kind man and no doubt realised how I struggled with some of the heavier spanners at first. He turned out to be an excellent teacher and I soon learned how to carry out my tasks under his guidance.

It was here that I learned how the depot operated and I watched as the great variety of engines came in for maintenance. There were 80 based at Wellingborough depot: shunt engines, passenger tanks, 4-4-0 Midland compounds, Classes 3, 4, 7 and 8 FRTs, and Garratts. The oldest was no. 251, a Class 1 passenger engine, but others passed through and I recall seeing a very early engine: no. 12, which was a Midland Class 2 freight 0-6-0 tender loco with the axle boxes set outside.

The terrible accident caused by a luggage truck in1898.

Jobs like removing the wheels from these engines had to be done the hard way in those days. In a corner of the big repair shed, on a long road from the turntable, stood a giant "Shear Legs" for lifting locomotives. Three massive wooden posts, at least 18" square, soared up to the roof of the shed, supporting a huge set of pulley blocks worked by a two-handle drum and ratchet. The engine would be parted from the tender and I used to watch in fascination as one end was slowly lifted upwards. It took at least half an hour's hard work by the two men on the drum handles before the engine was high enough for the wheels to be taken out. Later on, a new drop pit was built so that the wheels could be lowered from the engine into the pit and the engine hauled away. A hydraulic pump brought the wheels up and out of the pit again for inspection, making the whole process much easier and quicker and able to be carried out by one man.

But when I started work, things had not changed a great deal from my grandfather's time. Working conditions were rather better but methods of working had often been the same for many years. Certain improvements had been made and these had come about as the result of quite serious accidents.

On September 2nd 1898 the 7.15 p.m. express train from St Pancras came thundering through Wellingborough station on its daily journey to Manchester. As it roared past, an unattended luggage truck had rolled off the platform straight into the path of the train. The engine and first coach were

Above and below: this boiler explosion in 1900 led to improvements in safety.

derailed and the driver and fireman were killed. Following this accident the design of the luggage truck was changed so that it could not move on its own, thereby giving Wellingborough a place in railway history. There is no mention of any passenger casualties alongside the skilfully restored photograph that appeared many years later in the local newspaper, but the terrible damage done to the coach must have resulted in many injuries, if not deaths.

My father gave me some photographs that were taken in his father's time, of a huge locomotive boiler explosion which had occurred about a quarter of a mile from Wellingborough station. At the turn of the century, boilers and safety valves were not checked for safety and as long as they were working they were judged to be perfectly all right. This state of affairs continued until 1900 when there was a very serious accident. It is impossible to tell from the pictures what kind of loco it was because of the tremendous damage and the lack of markings on the tender. If the train crew were on or near the engine at the time they must have been killed. Generally, although they were not maintained, the valves worked quite well, but in this case there had been an undetected problem which allowed pressure to build until it resulted in a catastrophe. As far as I know it was the only explosion of its kind, but, without a doubt, the new and stringent regulations concerning boiler and safety valve maintenance and testing that were in place by the time I started work had been introduced after this.

Events such as these led to improvements in train and passenger safety, but for us workers a strong body and a sense of humour helped us to cope with long hours, hard, dirty work and a strict regime.

3 Workmates, boiler acrobatics and a runaway train

Rules were rules and I had to learn to be very punctual in the mornings. I was given a brass cheque, numbered 525, and this was used for clocking on. Everyone had one of these and they had to be put into a slot in the store-keeper's office. At two minutes to eight this man would start to ring a bell on the end of a rope and at precisely eight o'clock the slot was slammed shut. If you arrived with your cheque a few seconds later you were sent home, coming back in the afternoon for a telling-off and having already lost a day's pay. So it was not turning out to be an easy life, but I thrived on it. Going off to work with Dad I was as proud as punch and really felt this was where I belonged. I was happy when my workmates began to call me 'Jack'.

I began to get to know some of the characters I was to work alongside for the next 23 years. I can remember the face of the carpenter, disfigured by a bullet taken in the Great War. He was a good carpenter and I liked to watch him work, but his conversation centred wholly around horse racing and betting. As I could not pretend even a mild interest in either, we did not have much in common.

But I got on well with the coppersmith. He was a fiery little man with a huge handlebar moustache and he seemed to enjoy talking to me; I always felt our similar height had something to do with it. I knew when he was close by because he always gave off a rather unpleasant aroma. The poor man suffered from very painful joints and the smell came from the powerful oint-ment he used to ease the aches. One day the pain was so bad that he was allowed to go home. In those days most people walked or went to work by bicycle – there was no car park full of cars – and the coppersmith was not in a fit state to make the journey. So the poor man was taken home in a wheel-barrow. Since he lived a considerable way from the depot this couldn't have been a pleasant trip. But he recovered and was soon back, chewing his tobacco as he worked and catching people unawares as he spat the juice in all direc-tions. He was an interesting man, later awarded an MBE for his services to the St John's Ambulance Brigade.

At the opposite side of the spectrum was the blacksmith, a giant of a man who stared at his fire through great bushy eyebrows. He was not a man to be messed around with and everyone was well aware that he could bend a 6" nail with his bare hands, as if it were no more than a piece of wire. However, he and I got on well together and he taught me how to harden chisels and scrapers in the fire, waiting for the yellow and blue colours to appear and cooling off the metal at exactly the right moment. If he was away for any reason my father, who was quite a good blacksmith, used to stand in for him. I was proud of that.

One of the fitter's mates had been on the stage before he joined the railway. He had performed as a 'Strong Man' and he liked to remind us all of this by lifting me high above his head with one hand. I was scared to death, but of course I didn't dare show it. Some years after I first met him, this same man had one of those terrible accidents that can happen to people who work with any kind of moving machines. He was working in the shed, as he had many times, between an engine and tender. Another engine came along and just caught one of the other's buffers, causing it to roll forward into the tender. Very sadly, the man was crushed to death.

At the end of my first year I spent three months in the Foreman Fitter's office. This was very different work and most of my time I was writing out time books. I didn't mind too much but I could hardly wait to start getting my hands dirty again. And dirty they got – from now on my hands were never really clean again, such was the penetration of loco grime. Only when I had been on holiday for a week did they gradually regain their old colour.

Washing facilities were non-existent in the engine sheds. At the end of a shift we had to draw a bucket of hot water from one of the engines and do the best we could. Each week we were issued with a small tin containing soft soap, like a kind of jelly. We were also given six cloths: three new white ones and three washed ones. The white ones were for drying your face and head; the others for cleaning hands and tools while working. If your hands were really covered in soot and oil it was best to rub the first layer off with paraffin before using the soap and water.

In winter the hot water was welcome. The sheds were very cold and draughty and sometimes there was an inch or two of snow on the floors. Big funnels let out the smoke from the engines, and there was nothing to prevent the snow from blowing down through them. If the Garratts outside needed attention during a spell of bad weather, the tools would almost stick to our hands in the icy temperatures. The only thing to do was to work as hard and fast as possible to keep warm. A coal fire burned near the staff lockers so this gave a bit of relief from the cold if we managed to snatch a break. Railway rules being very strict, there was no such thing as an official break for tea or anything else during working hours.

A Garratt on the shed at Wellingborough in the 1930s

I was still small and this resulted in my often being chosen for jobs that most of the men would have found impossible. Removing the regulator valves deep inside the boilers was one of these. When this needed doing the tubers would be the first men on the scene, taking out about 20 tubes from the boiler so that there would be room for me to get my legs inside. Then I was called away from whatever job I was doing and told to slide in. Since my Dad was the boilersmith I couldn't really argue.

The four longitudinal stays had to be jacked open, exposing a gap of only about twelve inches for me to wriggle through. I had to lie along the tubes and remove the retaining nuts and pins that held the regulator valve. It felt very claustrophobic, deep inside there, and seemed a long way back to the opening. It was great to be on the outside again. Trouble was, the valve then had to be replaced and the journey repeated. Getting out the second time was the most difficult part because the valve restricted the space even more. What a relief when the job was done!

Of course I couldn't do it for ever and by the time I was seventeen I was too big for the hole. I remember the day another young apprentice was approached and persuaded to have a go. He started off well but then managed to get himself stuck in a rather awkward position. The poor lad panicked and went rigid with fright. It took a very long time and a great deal of gentle persuasion to get him out in one piece, and, to my knowledge, he never entered a boiler again.

Occasionally, unusual jobs came along; jobs that were much less worrying and far more fun. Not too far away from the sheds was a provender store. It was a massive five-storey building stacked all along its length on every floor with large sacks of grain. When they needed transporting, these sacks had to be lowered from floor to floor. The work was done by a very large gas engine. It had a flywheel, about eight feet in diameter, which powered a series of belt-driven pulleys. Sometimes, the engine's burner valve needed changing and the task fell to one of the fitters I was apprenticed to. He used to take me along when he did the job but, as he didn't really need me to help, I was allowed to roam freely while he worked.

I soon discovered that the store was completely overrun with rats, and I regarded this as a challenge. I used to wait quietly, weapon in hand, until I saw a movement in a sack, and then – quick as a flash of lightning – I was across the floor! One swipe with my iron bar and I reckoned I'd got it. Then, I'd go back to my fitter and tell him how I'd vanquished another of the enemy. An excellent way to spend a morning!

There was a lot of variety in the jobs that came our way so the days were never dull. Another of the fitters used to take me with him to attend to the 'Pull and Push' train. This train made several trips a day from Wellingborough to Rushden along a five-mile branch line. It could be operated from the coach as well as the engine so that there was no need to turn the train. A long wire for the whistle and pipes for the steam ran from the engine to the coach at the rear. This coach had a window and a seat for the driver who operated a steam valve and brake valve when he worked from this end.

When the train went to Rushden, the coach led. First, the fireman would get onto the engine, opening the steam regulator. Then the driver stepped into the coach and opened his steam valve. Off went the train, driven from the coach to Rushden and by the engine back to Wellingborough. Being so long, sometimes the whistle control wire would stretch and we had to readjust it. This was a nice little job, especially on a summer's day when we were able to travel with the train on one of its trips.

One day, the driver and fireman stabled the Pull and Push train in a siding near Wellingborough station for the night and left for home at about 10.30 p.m. Unfortunately, the fireman had forgotten to close the regulator on the engine. The driver had shut down the valve in the coach, but the steam pressure from the engine slowly became too much for it, and steam began to enter the engine cylinder. In the middle of the night, the whole train started to move and it travelled a mile, driverless, before it ran out of steam. Fortunately, it went up the branch line and no damage was done to anything or anybody. Of course the local newspaper, the Evening Telegraph, saw a good opportunity here and the following day this headline appeared:

GHOST TRAIN RUNS A MILE WITHOUT ANY TRAIN CREW

Needless to say, the driver and fireman were both in deep trouble that day.

In those days a train driver was held in great respect by the public, many of whom would have given their eye-teeth to swap jobs. To us who worked in the depot they were a breed apart and, to me, quite interesting characters. I can see in my mind a driver everyone knew as 'Ducky'. He had this nickname because he loved eating ducks' eggs. Between shifts he would cook himself an enormous meal of two huge eggs, bacon, sausage and anything else he'd crammed into his bag. I used to stare in amazement as he devoured the lot. Sometimes some of the men reminded Ducky of an old wives' tale that warned of 'something nasty' in the occasional duck egg. It was only supposed to occur in one egg out of a thousand but – yes, you've guessed it; one day, after eating one of these meals, the driver was taken ill. Shortly afterwards, he died.

4 Hard work in the machine shop

When I was about fifteen and a half years old I was sent to the machine shop so that I could learn to use the lathes, drilling machines and planers. This was real progress! The fitter in charge was a man called Joe, a good friend of my father. He was a clever chap and very pleasant to work with. I enjoyed being with him and learning all I could. I had to begin by cleaning all the machinery and making sure the floors were swept free of all the waste from metal turning. Soon, I made a start on little jobs on the lathe, such as 'facing up' small valves. This was followed by my first attempts at drilling and I began to really enjoy the work.

Before too long, I was brought back to earth with a bump. The person responsible for this was the Mechanical Foreman who ruled over us in the old way – with a rod of iron. He came into the shop one day and said, "Jack, I want you to clean and polish all the straight edges, and when you've done them, melt some thick grease and coat them with it to stop them going rusty."

The straight edges hung on a long frame on the wall. There were five: two were the length of an engine frame – at least 20 feet – and 4" wide and 3/8" thick. They were black, made of iron and as much as I could lift. It had been years since they were last cleaned, so after I'd collected some emery paper I made an enthusiastic start.

However, I soon realised that after a whole day spent in rubbing away, I'd made very little impression on the metal, and certainly there was not the shine I expected. My hands had already started to ache, but they were to get a lot worse. I stuck at it for a week before I decided I was satisfied with my work. I thought that, by now, the edges looked quite good, so I covered them with grease and hung them up again. When the foreman came in I told him the job was finished. He strolled over to where the straight edges hung along the wall and took a 6" rule from his pocket. Scraping a bit of grease off one edge with this, he turned to me and said, "That's no good. You'll have to start again."

Whether he saw the look on my face I will never know, because after this he turned on his heel and marched out of the shop. As for me, after a long week's hard rubbing and very sore hands, I could have wept. It took me half a day to get the grease off, ready to begin again. Eventually, after many more sheets of emery paper and a further week's work, the straight edges were cleaned to our Mechanical Foreman's satisfaction.

This foreman definitely seemed to have what I would describe as a sadistic streak in him; it showed in the various ways he devised to make sure we were never too comfortable. Although we were not allowed a break, sometimes the desire for a cup of tea simply overcame us. When this happened, one of us would run round to the mess room with the billycan and bring back a hastily made brew of tea, covered with a cloth. We would quickly put it out of sight, behind a lathe. But on occasion, it was obvious that our observant foreman had spotted the can-carrier. Almost as soon as the tea was in its hiding place he would pay us a visit, passing the time of day and talking in a very friendly manner. When the steam from the billycan was finally no more, he would bid us Good-day and leave us to our cold tea.

My skills were improving and one day a driver came along with a pair of garden shears. He asked if I would sharpen them for him. I was pleased to be of help and, although our 6" sandstone wheel was very worn and wobbled as it turned, I managed to get a reasonable edge on them. I took them to the driver who seemed very pleased; so pleased, in fact, that he gave me 6d. At this time I was giving all my wages to Mum and this was the equivalent of half a week's pocket money. I'd be able to buy at least three bars of chocolate. Riches indeed!

I continued to add to my knowledge and experience and by the time I was 17 I was placed with the fitters who carried out all the big examinations and repairs. Now I felt I was truly learning my job and my pay had risen to 13/4d a week. I continued to give all my pay to my mother until I was 20, when she bought my last coat and told me that from then on I could 'pay my own way'. But even now, at 17, my pocket money had increased considerably and, with my two friends Ron and Dick, I began to think about saving up for a holiday.

Every August, staff were given one week's holiday without pay, but were granted a pass for free rail travel to get them to their destination and back again. Our ambition was to hire a motor cruiser on the Norfolk Broads and we started saving 2/- or, if we could afford it, 2/6d a week. A year later we had £5 each and we were off! I didn't need my free pass because my father was now the proud owner of a Ford 8 car, and we had persuaded him to take us to Oulton Broad in style.

The week was magical! We were thrilled with our 18' boat. She was called *Robin* and had an Austin 7 engine. If we really opened her up she would do eight miles an hour – and use a gallon of petrol for that eight miles. We broke down once on Breydon Water near Yarmouth, but it was all part of the experience and we had a fabulous week. At the end of the holiday, Dad came to fetch us. Stopping outside a pub when we were halfway home he said, "We'll

Swabbing the deck on Robin, 1937.

have a break now. Perhaps you'd like to buy me a drink?" We looked in our pockets. Ron had a penny, I had 10d, and Dick had nothing left at all. So poor old Dad had to pay for our drinks as well as buying his own.

We had the taste for holidays afloat now and as our wages increased us three lads were able to aspire to even better boats, the best one being *Jacqueline*. Not only was she a slick 24 feet in length and capable of 12mph, she also had the very latest in on-board radios. We thought we were the Bees' Knees as we cruised along in the summer of 1938. The following year we thought we would aim even higher and we paid a deposit on a 34' cabin cruiser called *Challenger 34*, a real beauty. This holiday though, was not to be, because war broke out and ruined our plans along with the rest of the nation's. We wrote to the owner of the boat, concerned about our deposit. He said he could do nothing and asked that we leave the matter in abeyance. This we did, along with our 30/- which we never saw again.

About six months after my 18th birthday, I was given a mate and started carrying out my own tasks. Although it felt like very hard work at the time, I was mechanically inclined and had no trouble in coping with all the different jobs. I was a lot taller now, about 6 feet, and whilst my weight was only about 10 stones, I was quite strong. I could lift pistons, valves and connecting rods without too much trouble.

My first mate was elderly and wily. He used to enjoy sitting and cleaning joints and piston ring grooves. However, every time I needed him to help me lift a heavy cover or replace a piston he would say, "Sorry Jack – I shall have to go to the toilet." This was frustrating for me because I wanted to put up a good show against my fellow fitters. But it did help me to learn a number of tricks of the trade with a pair of pulley blocks.

By now I was earning 26/- a week and had reached the end of my apprenticeship.

After six years and seven months I became a fully-fledged fitter in March 1939.

5 Miniature locos and a fitter's war service

Just before the war my father and I took a trip to London. We had heard about a model railway exhibition and were interested to see the trains in miniature. We were indeed impressed, so much so that we decided to make a model of our own. It was to be a Royal Scot; a 3½" gauge coal-fired engine weighing about ½cwt and measuring 4'0½" in length.

There was a corrugated roofed shed in our garden and this was to be the workshop. We had no electricity at that time and would need to spend many hours working to intricate dimensions by gaslight. We set to work on the new project. Our main purchase was a treadle-powered 3½" lathe, and we found all the castings needed for the wheels, cylinders, gauge frames and so on from a firm called Bassett-Loake in Northampton. Everything else was made in the shed. The main frames were cut out; pistons and valves turned up; side rods and connecting rods fashioned and fluted along with bushes.

Dad was an excellent boilersmith and could work wonders with any piece of metal. He made the firebox to suit, along with the smoke box and all the necessary boiler and firebox lagging. As a fitter-turner, I could manage all the turning and screw-cutting for the wheels, axles, axle boxes and bushes, and I particularly remember working on the dome cover. Along with the dome itself, I had to screw-cut 32 threads to the inch inside and out. Cutting the inside was not too bad, but the cover needed a band of threads only ½" wide and doing this on a treadle lathe by gaslight was quite testing.

When war broke out, obtaining materials became more difficult and our progress was slightly restricted. Nevertheless, after three and a half years' work the model at last was ready for testing. The loco looked grand, all painted up in maroon and gold livery. We had a few problems making the boiler steam and water-tight, and getting the piston valves to hold steam. Copper, brass and steel were all tried with varying degrees of luck, but at last we succeeded with cast iron rings and the engine was working.

Our next project was more ambitious. Dad and I decided to tackle a 4-6-4 Halton tank engine, 5" gauge. The experience we had had making the *Royal Scot* stood us in good stead and we got on with this one quite quickly. It was fitted with slide valves which were easier to make and worked very well. After

Our wartime models: Royal Scot, 3½" scale 4.6.0 (above) and the Halton tank engine, 5" gauge 4.6.0 (below).

two years the engine was finished.

In order to test it properly we needed a test bed. To make this we took the angle irons from an old bedstead and fixed them to a wooden trestle. The irons were 6 feet long and to these we fitted brass rollers. The engine was placed on the test bed, its main driving wheels on the rollers and the bogie wheels on either side. We used smokeless fuel to get full steam up. At first, the engine threw out a little water but then, to our great delight, we were off! She was puffing away happily at about half-regulator and we were very proud of our latest achievement.

Now I was a fitter I began regular shift working: mornings, followed by afternoons and then nights. I didn't enjoy working this way; the morning shift started at 00.00 hrs on Sunday night and the night shift had finished at 8.00 p.m. on Saturday. But it would have been unthinkable to complain, so we just got on with it.

One of my first jobs was to strip the brake blocks and brake hangers from the pony wheels of the Garratt 2-6-6-2 locomotives. The Garratts were articulated, having the water tank at one end, the boiler in the middle and the rotary coalbunker at the rear. Each was about 90 feet long and weighed 100 tons. They were the most powerful locos on the railways and could pull 87 loaded wagons from Toton, Nottinghamshire, to London, returning with 120 empties which made the train almost half a mile long. Because of a design fault, the application of the brakes used to cause the pony wheels to lock and skid, resulting in 'flats' on the wheels. Our job was to remove the problem gear and it was found not to affect the overall braking, so this solved the problem.

A few months after I became a fitter, war was declared. We railway workers were not called to join the forces because we were needed to keep the system running, now more than ever. We were issued with a round badge, stamped with the words 'On War Service', our work being a 'reserved occupation'. I soon misplaced this badge after the war, but I still have my father's

much grander brass one from the First World War, issued to him in 1915, in his early days as a boilersmith.

Although we were not called to fight, Dad and I felt we must contribute to the war effort and could be found fire-watching at night if we were working days, and on Home Guard duties in the evenings. We took it seriously and were both made 'Corporal Automatic Weapons Instructors' on British Lewis guns and the American water-cooled Browning machine guns. I was also a

My father's War Service badge, issued in 1915.

member of the Auxiliary Fire Pump team at the depot and we became quite proficient, working together. In fact we won a prize, competing against other teams in a local contest. So with the shift work as well, the days were becoming all work and no play!

The shed and machine shop had to be blacked out at night. For this we made removable canvas shutters to fit all the windows. For the locos, canvas sheets were supplied to fit between engine and tender so that the glow from the fire could not be seen from above. Lights were not allowed in the sidings and no fires were permitted, so if your job for the day or night was outside there was only one option in icy weather: work hard to keep warm.

Near Wellingborough Control Offices, in Finedon Road sidings, was a road from which the footplate staff could clean out hot ashes from the loco-motive fires. This was done before and after shunting (moving wagons around a yard) and tripping (moving wagons from one yard to another) in the area. Over the years, the ash heap had grown to a length of about 20 yards and was about 8 feet high. Nearby was a signalbox, and one of the signalmen reported that, during the hours of darkness, the ash could be seen glowing red and might be spotted from the air. This would not do at all during wartime, so I was asked to go along with some members of the railway fire brigade to look and see if anything could be done.

We decided to take a little auxiliary fire pump with us and connect it to the tender tank of a locomotive so that we would have a water supply of 2,500 gallons. When we arrived we could feel the heat some yards away, but we could not see the fire which was deep down inside the ashes. I decided to use a long fire-iron from the loco to make a hole down into the middle of the heap. Then we started the pump and put the hose into the hole. The water caused steam to rise out of the hole, and this continued steadily for some minutes. Then suddenly, there was a loud cracking noise and the ground beneath our feet rumbled and shook. It was quite frightening but I knew I had to keep that water flowing in.

The noises continued for quite a few minutes, but, after several hundred gallons had flooded the ground, the rumbling and cracking gradually ceased. We left after an hour, thinking we had only just damped things down a bit, the seat of the fire being really deep in the ground. But we must have done some good because there were no more complaints, and during my years at Wellingborough I never heard it mentioned again.

Despite the changes brought about by the war, usually we managed to keep the trains running to order for the duration. This was not easy, because some of our locos had been bomb-damaged and others, that were being sent

An American WD locomotive sent to Wellingborough in 1942.

to Europe, had been sunk whilst at sea. We were getting short of engines. Help came in the form of some 2-6-0 locomotives which arrived from the USA. They had a similar working load to our Class 8 engines, but of course were different from the locos we were used to.

At first, we had quite a bit of trouble with them and problems to solve. The side rod and big end bushes on these engines were made of brass and this caused them to 'run hot' most of the time. Our solution was to take out the bushes, re-bore them and put in a white metal bearing, as in our own loco-motives. We also needed to replace the piston packing with our own material because the original packing let steam escape quite badly, resulting in complaints from the drivers. Once we had these two things sorted out the locos were put into regular use. What happened to them after the war ended I have no idea; they disappeared from the depot quite quickly.

During these wartime years life began to change for me. Although there was plenty to keep me occupied at Wellingborough I was suddenly needed elsewhere, and for the first time in my young life I had to work and live away from home.

6 War-time help at other depots

By February 1942 I had a new mate and a good friend, Alf, and he and I had been taking out and replacing wheels after hot axle repairs. For this work I was able to use our new wheel drop, which was a great improvement on the old Shear Legs and its drum handles.

Having become proficient in doing this, I was asked to go and do the same thing at Toton, the big Nottinghamshire railway depot, because it was very short of staff. My lodgings were just over the county boundary at Long Eaton in Derbyshire, and to get to work I had to walk about a mile through a shunting yard. It had 100 sets of lines side by side and, at the time, was one of the biggest in England.

To walk through here in complete darkness was a nerve-wracking experience. The wagons were pushed up a hump and then released to freewheel down into the selected siding. Although you could see nothing, you could hear them coming; sailing down the slope at full speed on any of the many lines. You knew one had found its home when an almighty bang told you it had finally hit the rest of the traffic on that line. Very luckily for me, I was never on the wrong line at the wrong time!

The engine sheds were very large and housed about 50 locomotives. There were no roofs on these sheds so we workmen were exposed to all weathers. One day we were working in at least six inches of snow and I left my tool bag on an engine while we had a sandwich. I remember going back to fetch it; I lifted it off the footplate and this very heavy bag was frozen solid. Although we needed to eat, having a break seemed to cause a problem that winter. The weather was bad – not the ideal time to be always out of doors.

Later that year I went to Leeds Holbeck motive power depot to help out in the sheds up there. They too were short-staffed and along with this, they had an unusual amount of engines with hot axles in for repair. Leeds was a long way from home and felt strange. It should have been easy to find lodgings in such a big city but there didn't seem to be many available rooms. I ended up in a decidedly large building, about five storeys high and having more than 300 rooms. My room, right at the top, was number 316. It had just a small bed and a locker, but did give me a wonderful view of Leeds from the window.

Down at the bottom of the hostel was the washroom and I learned very quickly to keep a careful eye on my property in there. On the second morning

I washed my face and bent down to rinse off the lather. As I straightened up to dry myself I noticed that my soap had disappeared. Looking around, all I could see was a row of innocent-looking individuals busy with their ablutions. For breakfast we were served curled-up kippers on toast and nearly-cold tea, so it was altogether a great start to the day!

After a week or so, I was able to move on. A fellow fitter, also relieving at Holbeck, was having similar problems and we both managed to get rooms in a back-to-back house nearer to our work. The houses had a block of lavatories in a yard at the end of the street, so we were given a key to the yard and a key to our toilet. I'll leave you to imagine what using this was like in the middle of the night in pitch blackness.

Here, I had to share a room with a Scotsman. I'd met very few Scottish people before and I found his strong accent made it very difficult for me to understand him. He was not aware of this and, although I tried to discourage him, he seemed to want to talk to me half the night, smoking cigarette after cigarette, and keeping me awake till the early hours of the morning. I was getting more and more tired through lack of sleep and working long days. However, one day he was at work using an acetylene cutter, chattering away as usual, when a spark flew straight into his open mouth and stuck itself on his throat. It was very painful for him, but I must admit it gave me a bit of peace for a while.

All in all, my stay in that little house was really quite eventful. On our second day there, the landlady was taken to hospital, so we were in the novel position of looking after ourselves. We managed this quite well, even the cooking. There was, though, a bit of a delicate problem with my fellow fitter. After our first seven to seven, 12-hour shift we arrived at the house, looking forward to relaxing. This fellow eased himself gratefully into a chair and said, "Sorry boy – I shall have to take them off." I didn't know what he meant at first, but 'them' turned out to be his boots. And he was quite right to warn me. I had never smelt anything quite like it. It was really bad and certainly didn't help our appetites at mealtimes. But of course, people didn't bathe or shower all the time in those days like they do now, so we just had to put up with it.

While I was in Leeds I had the pleasure of working on number 1000, a 4-4-0 Midland compound loco. The reason this was so special to me was that since I was about eight years old, we had had a framed picture of this very locomotive at home. I used to look at it and wish I could see it; now here I was working on it! My job was to change the tender brake blocks. They were made of wood and this engine must have been one of the last to have been fitted with this type of block. I'm sure you can imagine my delight when, visiting York

Midland Compound loco no. 1000.

Railway Museum with my wife nearly 40 years later, in 1981, I found myself looking once again at this engine, now restored to tip-top condition.

At this time, I had only been married to my wife, Kath, for a few months so I was looking forward to getting back home to Wellingborough. I had spent eight weeks in Leeds, fitting axle boxes to wheels and replacing wheels in the engines. The days were very long and there was little time to go out in the evenings. It was late in the year by now and bitterly cold. I remember how it felt to be walking home after dark in the blackout; the overhead wires from the trams suddenly flashing in the rain-soaked streets and frightening us young blokes half to death! It felt good to finally board the train for Northamptonshire.

In 1943 I was asked to help out again, this time at Plaistow in London. Once more, it was difficult to find a place to stay and I ended up with the depot's storekeeper and his family in West Ham. Their house had been badly damaged during bombing raids and I can see now their Rexine (mock leather) three-piece suite. It had been so badly cut by flying glass from the windows that all the packing protruded through the slits. Despite the conditions they lived in and the ever-present threat of attack they lived with, they were very happy people and coped really well with the almost nightly sirens and air raids. The son was a lighter-man on a Thames barge and went out every evening to the pub where his father was a barman and his mother played the piano. They weren't prepared to let a thing like war put paid to their fun!

It was about this time that Germany was running short of aeroplanes, just before her leaders started concentrating on fly-bombs and rockets. On my second night in London, 240 planes were sent over in a last-ditch effort. Apparently one of their main targets was the Mulhard Valve factory which was about a mile away from us.

Chandelier flares and searchlights lit up the sky. Anti-aircraft guns were kicking up a terrible racket, and to go outside was to risk falling shrapnel which was smashing roof tiles and greenhouses all around us. The main reason for this was 76 rockets based on West Ham football ground, all of them being fired together and shooting into the sky with a roar like an express train. The aim of these rockets was to create a blanket of anti-aircraft shells a quarter of a square mile up in the target area, but although I saw quite a few planes caught in the searchlights, I failed to see one brought down.

I spent two periods of several weeks here, the second time being rather more difficult than the first. I was given a work-shy apprentice who seemed to do more harm than good on those occasions when he did manage to pull his finger out a bit. This meant that the work was completed nowhere near quick enough for the newly-promoted mechanical foreman. This man's main interest seemed to lie in building up a fierce reputation by acting tough. Years later, we met on much more equal terms, but at that time it made our working relationship difficult and I was glad when we could part company. Nevertheless, it had been a valuable experience and gave me a real insight into what Londoners had to cope with in wartime.

Although I was sent to other places, we were short of fitters ourselves and I remember four great chaps coming over from Northern Ireland to help at Wellingborough depot. They worked hard at repairing engines but, since their previous jobs had been in making electric fans, they didn't find it easy to cope with the change to much heavier work. It was also very dirty, oily and sooty and their inexperience seemed to make them much dirtier than everyone else. After they'd been working in the smoke box, in which there was always a thick layer of soot, you could only tell who was who by their voices and the whites of their eyes! At the end of the war three of the men went home to Ireland but the fourth married a local girl and settled down in Wellingborough.

When peace was declared and the war was finally over, everything slowly came back to normal. By this time my wife and I had a new baby girl to think about and I was happy that I was reasonably good at my job. Life was going along quite nicely – but I didn't want to stand still!

7 Joining the breakdown crew and a chance to drive!

I was now one of only three fitters in the depot who could set valves on the locomotives to ensure that they steamed properly and gave maximum performance when hauling heavy trains. Wanting to improve myself, I became proficient at acetylene cutting and welding. I had an ulterior motive for doing this; I was mad keen to be selected for the Breakdown Crew: a team of eight men who could be called upon at any time to attend to derailments or carry out lifting work with the steam crane. It meant extra money of course, so the competition was fierce. There was an extra four shillings for each call-out, plus the overtime from the breakdown itself. Because the pay was so attractive it took me another two years before I finally made it. But the experience was to stand me in good stead later, when I got promotion to the salaried and supervisory grades.

So now I was part of the motley crew. As a fitter, my job was to carry out any work required on the locomotive, such as parting the engine from the tender and examining after re-railing to ensure it was fit for travelling. The gang consisted of the blacksmith and his striker, two of us fitters, a tuber and three fitter's mates; two of them trained as crane drivers and one as the cook. When I first joined the railway, the only food given to a member of the breakdown crew was a large dry biscuit and a cup of Bovril. By the time I was part of things new regulations stated that the men must have a hot meal every four hours, so it was the cook's job to provide this.

As well as the changes to food, by the 1940s the general conditions for the breakdown crew were much improved. When I was a young apprentice I wouldn't have been so keen to join. The gang had hydraulic water jacks and windlass jacks. The water jacks used to freeze in the winter and the windlass jacks were very awkward to operate. These latter were used for lifting wagons. Basically, there was just a screw and a cog and a handle needing two men to turn it. If the jack or the wagon slipped at all, the jack would shoot out and the handle would fly off, putting the men in danger. Eventually, these were scrapped and replaced by bigger and stronger oil jacks, a much safer option.

When news of a breakdown reached the depot, the man known as the 'caller-upper' would cycle round the town, often in the dead of night, startling

Fitters and mates in 1946. I'm at the back on the right.

a sleeping family with a loud rat-tat. Whereupon the man of the house would stumble out of bed and down the stairs to open the front door and find out what kind of job he was needed for. Then, it was a case of pulling on some clothes, getting out the bicycle and, in my case, being thankful I didn't live far from the depot. When I was on duty the caller-upper's job fell to me. This, of course, had to be done in all weathers and at any time of the day or night. One of the gang members lived about two miles from the depot and, every time I arrived at his darkened house, he would only speak to me through the letterbox!

We had many derailed wagons in our large sidings at Wellingborough, but by far the worst time I spent on a job was during a winter's night in a little sidings adjacent to Whitworth's Flour mill, about 3 miles from our depot. The breakdown train had been called to a derailment at Kettering but only half the normal crew was required, so I had stayed behind. When the call came in from the mill it was about 2.00 a.m., bitterly cold and snowing heavily. Apparently the derailed wagon was required urgently and my mate and I were the only workers available. We started preparations for the job. Collecting two jacks, some wooden packing and a Tilly lamp, we loaded them onto a Class 4 FRT loco.

Half an hour later the driver brought the engine to a stop at the site. Picking up the Tilly lamp, I jumped off the loco – and landed directly into 3 feet of snow, the lamp almost disappearing. This meant that, in order to find the wheels that had come off the rails when they hit the snowdrift, the first thing we had to do was to dig. We were wearing just our boiler-suit overalls, and, although after digging down, we soon got the job done, there was a biting wind and our bare hands were stiff with cold. But we were yet to feel even colder. Driving out here we'd travelled 'engine first', so going back meant 'tender first'. The engine had given us some protection on the first journey but on the return we were completely exposed to the driving snow and cutting wind for half an hour. By the time we arrived at the depot we felt, and looked, absolutely frozen. The coal fires had never seemed so welcome.

I can't be exact, but I think it was about 1948 when the breakdown crew was called to a very serious derailment at Oakham in Bedfordshire. We were shocked to learn that both the Wellingborough driver and fireman had been killed when their freight train had hit the rear of a stationary train, right in the middle of a very high bridge. The Class 8 FRT 2-8-0 engine and its three wagons, loaded with coal, had smashed through the wall of the bridge, falling about 40 feet into the field below – just missing the nearby river. We hauled

The fatal accident at Oakham, 1948.

the wagons back up onto the bridge, loaded them up again and had them taken away, but the loco was another matter.

It had come to rest on its side, half-covered in coal, and was difficult to get at. Also, it was too heavy for our 36-ton crane, because it weighed something like 75 tons. Our job, therefore, was to make it liftable. After moving many tons of coal we decided to part the engine from the tender and strip it of all movable parts. We took off the side rods, connecting rods, slideblocks and as many other parts as possible until, finally, the boiler was ready for lifting from the engine frames. Luckily, the weather was very kind to us, for it was a big job and had taken us three days of hammering and cutting to get this far. Finally, the engine, in all its pieces, was lifted the 40 feet back up to the bridge. Here, it was placed directly onto special low wagons, its destination being either Derby works or the scrapyard.

It was about this time that I realised every boy's dream: to drive a steam engine! One of our Class 3P 2-4-0 passenger engines had been having steaming problems, with a lack of power when pulling a loaded train. My foreman fitter suggested that if we removed a cast iron protrusion in the blast pipe this might solve the problem. The work took about a day to complete, and a couple of days later the foreman arranged for me to travel with the engine on a local Wellingborough to Bedford train. This would let me see what effect, if any, my work had had on the overall performance of the train. The passengers climbed aboard and I stood on the footplate with the driver. The train ran well, and after about five miles he turned to me and said, "Come on then Jack, you have a drive!"

Well, what an opportunity! Under his supervision, I actually drove the train for the next five miles – a wonderful but nerve-wracking experience, especially at 60mph. Just as well the trusting passengers had no inkling of this!

It was a good tale to tell Dad, who also had something to tell me. He had been Chargehand Boilersmith for some time, and now a new post of Area Foreman Boilersmith had been created. This was a salaried position and he had been selected for the job. He had responsibility for all the boiler work in the Wellingborough, Bedford, Leicester and Kettering areas and took it all in his stride, managing very well until he retired in 1952 after 50 years' continuous service on the railway. In fact my father, grandfather and I knocked up a century of uninterrupted railway service for our family.

In 1949 we had a very big job at the depot. An engine had run into the turntable well which was about 6 feet deep. It was about four in the afternoon and the engine had stood on a middle road in the heavy repair shed, fired up and ready for work. Unfortunately someone had left the regulator open slightly and the tender brake was not fully screwed on. Added to this was the fact that the engine had been left in forward gear. When steam pressure began to build, naturally the engine started to move forward of its own accord and, before we knew it, the front part ended up with its leading and driving wheels in the well. The front buffers were only about a foot short of the turntable itself.

The event paralysed the whole shed. It was 'all hands to the pumps' and we started jacking and packing, gradually lifting up the engine. This took every piece of wood in the breakdown train and all the spare sleepers we could find. Eventually we had a platform six feet high. Then we jacked again, putting steel plate under the wheels, ready to move the engine back onto the road from whence it came – a distance of about 20 feet. Moving it was not easy because we had no other means of shifting it except to crowbar it back, bit by bit. It took hours. We finally went home at 1.30 a.m. after another hour and a half spent clearing up all the tackle and packing.

By this time I was beginning to get fed up with working three shifts all the time, not least because I found it difficult to sleep in the daytime. The shift that started at midnight on Sundays was particularly bad. Apart from spoiling your weekend, when you arrived at work the locos had all been fired up during the evening and the shed was full of thick yellow smoke. About 12 firelighters had been used for each engine. These caused a heavy smog which never really cleared until about 4.00 a.m., by which time you knew how a kipper felt! Fortunately, a vacancy came up for a third fitter/turner in our machine shop. This interested me and the shifts were only one week in three. It was 1950 when I put in a successful application and started my new job which, by now, would be with British Railways, the LMS having been nationalised on 1st January 1948.

8 Fitter/turner in the machine shop

The old machine shop had just been replaced when I started work there. The new shop had been fitted out with a planing machine, a drilling machine, two lathes – one 12" and the other 24", an emery wheel and a massive wheel and journal turning machine with 7'6" faceplates. There were new benches, an anvil, and the coppersmith's corner with all the equipment for bending pipes, and white metal melting bowls for the re-metalling of axle boxes, big ends and bushes. The coppersmith would re-metal these items as they came in and then we fitter/turners would set them up in the big lathe, go to the wheels and measure the journals, then re-bore and face, ready for the fitters to refit and replace on the wheels.

Piston and piston valves had to be placed in the lathe and highly polished, and new gland packing bored out to the appropriate size in the smaller lathe. Big end bolts, which were about two feet long, had to be turned out of rough castings, tapered and screw-cut for a 1½" nut. All the different brass water valves used on the locos were refaced. Large crossheads and slideblocks were all planed to fit after re-metalling. So there was plenty of work to keep us busy.

One of the hardest jobs was to lift wheels and set them up in the wheel lathe when they were brought in for turning. We lifted them by means of chain blocks, each pull on the block raising the 1½ ton wheels by a quarter of an inch. By the time they were two feet off the ground and high enough to be propelled into the lathe – about twenty minutes in all – you were just about exhausted. Then the wheels had to be clamped to the faceplate by using cast-iron sleeves, which weighed about 30 lbs. They were in turn clamped to onto four spigots. These needed to be screwed up securely against the wheel through the spokes, and packed tightly with wooden packing, put in with a 7 lb hammer. The whole process of getting a wheel ready for turning took about one and a half hours.

The trickiest job in the wheel lathe was the turning up of the axle journals, especially when the wheels concerned had driving wheels with 18" cranks. Because of the cranks it wasn't possible to make a full cut straight across the journal and it had to be done in two halves. The art lay in getting the second cut exactly right, when picking up from the first. This was vital because the two halves had to be polished together to a perfectly level surface to finish off the job.

A wheel lathe at Swindon Steam Railway Museum in 1990, similar to but smaller than ours which had 8' faceplates.

When the steel tyre treads of a wheel began to wear and needed turning, a ½" cut was set and the traverse switched on. It took an hour for the cut to go right across to the tyre flange, after which it was re-shaped with a special cutting tool in the exact shape of the completed flange. One night, I went over to check how the cut was going and watched the blue, hot steel cuttings peeling off in rings as they always did. However, as I was about to turn away, the button tool must have hit a hard spot on the tyre and I saw a ½" ring of steel cutting, smoking hot and flying towards my left eye. It seemed as if things were happening in slow motion and I just managed to close my eye in time. The cutting was stuck in the corner of my eyelid and was burning like mad, so it was Hobson's choice: either let it go on burning my eye or burn my fingers. I chose the fingers and pulled it out. My eye was very painful for some days afterwards. Of course this would never have happened had we been issued with protective glasses, but things like that were not an option in those days.

One of the more unusual jobs that came my way, and something else that wouldn't happen now, was the making of an ashtray for the boss's desk. I used an exhaust injector brass cap for the base, and halved a piece of ½" steel piping to hold the burning cigarette. I thought this was quite inventive and when finished it must have weighed a couple of pounds, so no doubt it was also very useful as a paperweight!

It's worth mentioning some of the varied tools we used in the maintenance of steam locomotives. We had a huge range of ring and open-ended spanners, ranging from ½" up to 2½". After the 1" size, all were very solid and heavy, having a thickness of at least an inch; the 2½" spanner was five inches across the jaws and about three feet long. It was used for adjusting the brakes on Class 8 and 9 FRT locos and, as it had to be used in the confined space in the engine pit beneath the locomotive, the job was very awkward and heavy. There were dozens of box spanners of all sizes; tommy bars; hammers from 1½ lbs to 28 lbs; and drills from ½" to 2" in diameter. Then there were punches; chisels; round-nosed tools; and files which were round, square, flat, triangular or half-round, and ranging from six inches to two feet in length.

We used a very large clamp, weighing about 60 lbs, for squeezing the engines and tenders together. This enabled the drawpin to be taken out so that an engine and tender could be parted for repair and examination. We also had 7 feet long pinch bars as levers under the wheels of locomotives, to move them along when they were out of steam. Using these enabled two men to move a 75-ton loco a short distance on the engine roads in the shed. 25-ton hydraulic jacks were used for lifting the locos when we needed to change the main wheel springs, which weighed 2cwt each.

Then there were cutting tools for the refacing of the brass seatings in injection and return valves for boilers; a hydraulic press for removing and replacing side rod and connecting rod brass bushes; and all sizes of taps and screw-cutting equipment for re-threading bolts and nuts from ½" to 1½". For lifting out valves, pistons and the like, there were both chain and pulley blocks.

Most of these tools were kept in a shed. They were looked after by a fitter's mate whose job it was to ensure that what went out came back in good order so that he could clean it before it was needed again. Most had been there for some years and I knew they would still be there, held by many different hands, long after I had left the depot.

And I had begun to think about moving on. I had enjoyed my time in the machine shop, although it was 'all go' from the start and became even busier during my last year. This happened because the coppersmith retired and I took over his duties as well as my own. I became fairly proficient in metalling, pipe-bending and brazing, so it added another string to my bow. But, although my shifts were now only one week in three, it still took me several days to get over the week of nights, and I was getting to the stage where I felt there was not a great future in carrying on as a fitter.

We had a salaried job vacancy sheet posted in our notice case and I'd seen the Shedmaster's job at Market Harborough advertised a couple of times in the past four years. And here it was again: a Class 3 post with regular day working and only 17 miles from Wellingborough so there would be no need to move house. It would suit me well and I sent in my first application.

I say 'first' because it took me two years of applications to get an interview finally in February 1955. I began to study and gather as much information about the post as I could, before going to Rugby to be interviewed by the District Motive Power Superintendent. Despite my hard work, it was all very strange and I felt as nervous as a kitten. This was my first venture outside the mechanical section of the railways and, although in the end I seemed to have a reasonably good interview, I never really thought I stood a chance of getting the job.

Two weeks later, however, a letter came, summoning me to the boss's office at Wellingborough. I went straight there and he told me I'd got the job and was to be 'a good lad, and not let the side down'! I really could not believe my luck. I started shaking like a leaf and wondering whether I'd done the right thing in planning to leave the sheds where I'd spent the last 23 years of my life.

I spent two more weeks in the machine shop and then, just after my 37th birthday, the day arrived for me to start my new job. Here, I was to meet my staff of 84 men in a strange depot, and to be Shedmaster in charge of many who were older than myself and more experienced in their side of the job than I was.

9 Shedmaster at Market Harborough

It was a big day when I stepped into my own office for the first time. It was an 8 feet square prefabricated hut adjoined to the mess room and locker room. Heating was provided by a little gas fire, and, on wet or damp days, the condensation was such that water would run down the walls and soak about six inches into the edges of the carpet. But it was mine, along with a tiny shed that held a wooden storeroom, a turntable and a water-softening plant. During my first week, the storekeeper fell sick and, although I never saw him again, he was not replaced. So I had his job to do whilst I was learning how to run the depot.

My working life began to change completely. I soon realised what a complex job management would be, and one requiring a great deal of patience and understanding. It took at least nine months for me to begin to feel comfortable in the post, and to gain confidence in myself as the person in charge. There were, for instance, some very young and cheeky engine cleaners at the depot who needed watching every minute. One day, I got so annoyed with them that I sent them home without pay – but then got into trouble with my boss for doing so! It did teach them a bit of a lesson though and their behaviour was quite a bit better afterwards.

I had to settle a row between the coalmen at the depot when one accused the other of 'cobbing' all the time and leaving all the hard work to him. The coal wagons were on a ramp, level with the engine tenders, and the coal had to be shovelled and thrown from wagon to tender, about a ton at a time. It was very hard work. To make his life a bit easier, one of the men would throw all the large lumps off the top of the wagon-load, leaving the other to shovel all the small cobbles from the bottom. In other words, he was 'cobbing', and it was much easier throwing these large lumps than shovelling. So it was down to me to have words with the culprit and put him right for the future. Although I managed to sort it out, I found this kind of thing very difficult at first because it was completely new to me.

As well as running the depot, keeping the peace and looking after the stores, I wanted to smarten up the place a bit so that it would give the impression of a clean, well-run depot. Hence I was soon squeezing in other jobs like painting the bicycle sheds. It was also still my job to carry out repairs and examinations of engines and I used to keep some boots and overalls in the

Market Harborough shed, 1961. Photo K.C.H. Fairey.

office for this. So, if an engine needed attention, it was often a quick change and then maybe into the tank!

One of my first vital duties at the depot was to find out why a considerable amount of brass and copper seemed to go missing after engines were stabled at Market Harborough shed overnight. Oil boxes, sandpipe nozzles and copper piping would all disappear. I first noticed it when an engine failed about two miles from the depot with a hot big end. The big end brasses needed to be retained at Rugby for inspection, but when I went to pack them up for sending away they were missing, although they weren't small and would have weighed about 12 lbs each.

I searched the depot, hunting everywhere and even draining cesspits, but without success. Other things kept disappearing and it was obvious that they had been doing so for some time. Eventually, after asking a lot of questions, everything seemed to point to my night chargehand who had been working regular nights for years. The railway police were contacted and made a search of his house – where they hit the jackpot! There were sacks bursting with brass and copper, tilley lamps and clothing. The man must have had quite a well-established little business because, when the police raided a scrap dealer's premises in the town, they found two further sacks of railway engine material.

When questioned, the dealer denied all knowledge of it and said he had no idea how it had got there. He and the chargehand were taken to court, where the dealer said he knew nothing of either the railwayman or his job, having never met him before, although it was common knowledge in the town that the two had been friends for years. Consequently, the scrap dealer got clean away with it because nothing could be proved. The chargehand, however, was fined heavily and lost his job. There had been quite a drama in court when his current wages were revealed. His wife, who was sitting next to me, jumped up and shouted, "He told me he only earned half of that – he must have spent it on drink!" The magistrate had to persuade her to sit down and be quiet.

Two months later we had the 1955 Railway Strike; a bad situation, as the NUR members were working and those from ASLEF were on strike because of differentials in pay for the footplate grades. Unfortunately the membership at this depot was split evenly between the two unions. This resulted in a lot of trouble between the two sides, with constant abuse from the pickets who were on the gate at the top of the depot.

About a week into the strike, a driver moved a shunt engine. The engine had been standing in the depot for some time, and this inactivity caused condensed water to collect in the cylinders. When an engine was moved this water would shoot straight up and out of the chimney, taking with it a fair amount of water-logged soot. On this day, the wind happened to be blowing in the direction of the white-shirted strikers who sat in a line along the fence by the gate. The driver had given the shunt engine quite a hefty regulator opening to clear the cylinder, and – within seconds – all the white shirts were covered in soot.

Inevitably, the driver's deed was misinterpreted and seen as a deliberate act against the strikers. Straight away, a stream of angry men in spotty shirts poured down the path to the depot, all seeking revenge. It was pandemonium for a while and took some time before what passed for normality at the time to be restored.

Eventually, the strike came to an end and I arranged to meet the former strikers on a Sunday morning in their club in the town. Here, I was to tell them which shifts they would be working when they resumed duties. It was not a pleasant task, punctuated with shouts of, "I'm not working with that scab!" and so on. On the Monday, when normal work started once more, the atmosphere in the mess room could have been cut with a knife. Quite a few arguments broke out but, apart from one fight during a night shift, things began gradually to settle down. It had been a very trying time.

Sorting out mechanical problems was a bit less trying, but nevertheless challenging. Two of the locomotive complement at the depot were 0-8-0 Class 7 FRT Western type locos which we used for banking trains on the

Market Harborough to Rugby line. The line ran through a single bore tunnel that was at least half a mile long and on a pretty steep uphill gradient. This meant that any reasonably heavily-loaded freight train running to Rugby had to have assistance to cope with this gradient. A bank engine was needed to push at the rear of the train until it had cleared the tunnel and reached the top of the slope.

We had problems with one of the seven freight locos used for this. The engine would stand behind the train looking fine; ready to go with a full head of steam and safety valves blowing their heads off. However, after pushing away at the train for four or five miles, the boiler would start to lose steam pressure very quickly, leaving the engine unable to provide the power needed to see the train through the tunnel. It got so bad that on one occasion the freight train actually left the bank engine standing.

Consequently, I was instructed by my superintendent at Rugby to ride on the bank engine while it was pushing to see if I could find out what was causing the loss of pressure over such a short time. So off we went on a bright summer's day with everything going well – the bank engine pushing hard at the rear of the train, and the fireman doing his best to keep a good clean fire.

As we approached a point within about half a mile of the tunnel, the boiler pressure began to plummet and we were struggling to keep proper assistance going for the train. Smoke and steam from its engine were already pouring out of the tunnel when we entered it, the train engine working hard to keep going fast enough to climb the uphill gradient. Once inside the tunnel, the walls and roof were only about 18" away from our engine and its smoke and steam were hammering on top of us and pouring down all around us. Everywhere was pitch-black and it was getting difficult to breathe while standing up. When the engine finally forced its way out into daylight the driver, fireman and myself were all down on the floor, trying to get our breath after gasping our way through the tunnel.

The train soon left us, as our engine was almost out of steam, having been of little use during the latter part of the banking effort. We remained stationary for a while to get more steam up so that we could return to the depot. Of course, this meant going back through the tunnel which was still pouring out its contents! It was a very smoky journey and would have been hard on anyone with breathing problems. I doubt that, in this present day and age, any staff would attempt a similar job without breathing apparatus.

Back at the depot, I had a good look at the engine and could see no leakage of any kind. It seemed to be in good mechanical order so I could only conclude that the boiler must be at fault. Most probably it was in need of a good B.C.O. (boiler clean out), as the water in our area was noted for causing limescale build-up. This was done and it did the trick.

10 Relieving at Northampton and an unexpected move

After 12 months of hard work, and a lot of time spent learning at my own expense from my mistakes, I was asked to relieve at Northampton, a fairly highly graded depot with some 350 staff and 50 locos. I was there for four months because the resident shedmaster had broken his wrist. The time was relatively uneventful, although I felt I learned a lot by keeping my eyes open and my mouth shut! Nevertheless, a couple of happenings stuck in my mind.

The first was an argument between the driver and fireman of a passenger train. Apparently, the fireman had left the doors of the firehole open after he'd finished shovelling coal into the firebox. The driver, noticing this, promptly shut them. This didn't please the fireman. A full-blown row instantly developed about whose job it was to attend to the firebox doors during the course of their duties.

At the time of the argument, the train was approaching Althorpe Park station. This was the halt for Lord Spencer's house and other important dwellings in the area, so the train could often be carrying VIPs. Things had become so heated that, as soon as they had pulled into the station, the fireman abandoned the driver, leaving him stranded with a train full of passengers. The driver was unable to proceed until a replacement fireman could be driven over to him in a taxi. As well as inconveniencing a large number of passengers, the stoppage held up other trains on the line.

Pretty soon, my telephone was red-hot. My boss from Rugby was very angry indeed and demanded to see the errant fireman as soon as he arrived back in Northampton. By the time the fireman had travelled by bus from Althorpe my boss was there, steam coming out of his ears and demanding an immediate explanation for the man's actions. The fireman looked at him steadily and said, "It's no good you shouting at me – I'm resigning forthwith." With that, he walked out of the office and we never saw him again. My boss's face was a picture of boiling anger and frustration and I was greatly relieved to see him off, back to Rugby.

Secondly, I remember I had a little cooling plant attendant at Northampton, who was a very good and conscientious worker. One day, he came to me and said, "Would you come and have a look at this? I think we've got a fault up the top."

I followed him to the cooling plant and we climbed five flights of stairs. At the top he called me over and I joined him at the edge of the platform. There was no handrail, and he pointed at something over the side. I looked down in the direction he was indicating and found my self staring down a sheer drop of about 150 feet. I almost overbalanced in my fright and I could think of nothing but breathing carefully and creeping gingerly away from that edge so that I could get back down to earth. I never did see what the man was pointing at. After we had descended and I'd finished shaking, I called the appropriate department to attend to the fault – whatever it was!

I did have a pleasant surprise during my time at Northampton. I was just hurrying to catch my train back to Wellingborough at Castle Street station, when I almost collided with the entertainers, Laurel and Hardy. No doubt they had been giving a show in the town. They had been very popular for years and it was a real thrill to see them in the flesh, although by now they were getting on in age and Oliver Hardy, carrying a lot of weight, was not walking well.

While I was at Market Harborough, in 1956, I had to relieve the shed-master at Nuneaton, in Warwickshire, two or three times. During one particular fortnight, I was called out to derailments in the shunt yards on 11 nights out of 12. Diesel shunt locos were used to push rafts of wagons slowly up a steep gradient called The Hump. When the wagons reached the top they were allowed to run freely down the other side, and then distributed into their various sidings by staff setting the rail points as necessary. On some roads the wagons had to be slowed down, either because it was a short siding or the road was already nearly full of wagons.

This was done using a steel tapered slipper. It was placed on the rail to slow down or skid the wheels, shooting out just as the wagon reached the points. That was the theory. But in reality the method was very 'hit and miss'; for every wagon slowed, one would be derailed and, of course, the breakdown crew were called out to clear up the mess. No wonder the regular shedmaster was often away from work – the poor chap hardly had a night in bed! Later on, the track was fitted with a hydraulic braking system which was very successful. I imagine the man was greatly relieved.

In September of that year, I was shaving one morning when the mirror in my rented bedroom began to move. Then, for a few seconds, the whole house shook. Never having experienced an earth tremor, I began to think I'd imagined it. But when I arrived at work the staff had heard that we had had an earthquake, level 5.6 on the Richter scale. Not severe, but quite a surprise for Warwickshire.

The following April, my boss asked me if I'd go to Barrow-in-Furness to replace the shedmaster, who'd been promoted to Chester. It would be just until another appointment had been made. This was at 5.00 p.m. on a Friday. I said yes, I would go as I thought the experience would stand me in good stead if I were to apply for promotion again. My boss said, "Right, I want you to go on Monday."

This left me very little time to tidy up at Market Harborough and tell the family that I'd be away to Barrow on Monday. I had never even heard of this place and when I looked at the map I had quite a shock to find that it was about 230 miles from Wellingborough, being, as it was in those days, in Lancashire. However, after rushing around after my tickets, packing a few belongings and finding a suitable train, Monday afternoon saw my arrival at Barrow station.

The station itself looked surprisingly modern to me. I soon discovered that this was because it had had to be rebuilt after the war, having suffered heavy bombing, like much of the town. The first station was built in 1882 after the old Furness Railway, originally built for iron ore and steel traffic, had laid a new line from Dalton to Barrow. The famous Furness loco *Coppernob* was still standing near the station when I stepped off the train, but would soon be removed and finally housed at the National Railway Museum in York. As well as many different steam locomotives, the company built a number of ships including the steam yacht *Gondola* which was restored by the National Trust in the 1970s and is still used for trips on Coniston Water. When I arrived, the Furness Railway had been part of the LMS since 1922.

Fortunately, arrangements for lodgings had already been made, and that evening I was able to move in with an elderly couple in Blake Street. I had a quick chat with the retiring shedmaster, who was on his last day at Barrow, and started work the next day. At that stage, I didn't know that I wouldn't be going back to Market Harborough again, and I got stuck into the job; getting to know the staff and finding my way around the area. But after five weeks my new boss came over from Carnforth, conducted a very short interview, and gave me the job of Shedmaster, Barrow-in-Furness.

It must have been a record summer; the sun shone almost daily. I borrowed an old 'caller-upper' bicycle from work and, every evening and on alternate weekends when I was not going home, I explored my surroundings. I cycled all round Walney Island, along the coast and around the busy docks, bustling with the town's ship-building industry. Coming from the Midlands

Pettigrew locomotives of the old Furness
Railway at Barrow M.P.D. ------ 1919

Furness Railway "Jumbo" Tank Locomotive
at Platform 2, Barrow Central, about 1921

Furness Railway locos.

this was all new and fascinating to me. Also, it meant that I got to know my way in and around Barrow, ready for when I moved into the town with my family. I found a house for sale just along the road from my lodgings in Blake Street, and we moved in August. It was quite hard for us to leave Northamptonshire but once done we felt as if we were on holiday, what with the glorious weather, and the sea and the Lake District right on our doorstep. We soon settled in, finding the people of Barrow warm and friendly.

11 Breakdowns and boats – a busy time by the sea

I had a staff of 250 and there were 56 locos, consisting mainly of 8 FRT, 4 FRT, half a dozen passenger tank engines and shunt engines. My small office overlooked the docks, and, just below the window, the aircraft carrier Hermes was undergoing a refit which was to take nearly three years. About half a mile away, Britain's first nuclear submarine, Dreadnought, was being built. In fact, if you looked over the bridge to Vickers Island during this period, you would see that Barrow docks were almost full of destroyers and frigates being repaired or refitted.

This was a very busy time for me; learning the area, getting to know all the staff and the motive power depot with its machine shops, coaling plants, ash plants and offices. At this time, 'work study' was being introduced to the

Barrow-in-Furness motive power depot in 1959.

railways and one of my first visitors was the Chief Officer for the Promotion of Work Study Procedures on the London Midland Region. He sounded very grand, but imagine my pleasure when it turned out to be Bill Thorley, a fellow apprentice from Wellingborough! And I bumped into him again a year or two later, on a course at the Derby School of Transport.

About two months after my arrival, on one of the rare, very wet days of that summer, we were called out to an incident at Lindale, about 12 miles from Ulverston. There, at the end of a little slip road off the main line, was a 50 foot turntable, stuck halfway round with a 60 ton 0-6-0 Class 4 FRT engine on it. The main centre support, which was a pivot – a long brass casting which rested on a brass ball about a foot in diameter – had collapsed. This allowed the whole structure to rest on the outside wheels. With no centre support to take the weight of the turntable, the whole thing seemed immovable. We decided to try jacking up the table so that we could move it a bit at a time, first one side and then the other, until the rails finally lined up.

The rain was coming down in buckets and the work was painfully slow. There was no base in the turntable pit, just bare earth and a few stones. After two hours we were working in about four inches of mud and water. Conditions became worse and worse but, after four nerve-wracking hours – with the cast iron outside supporting wheels cracking and shooting pieces of metal across the pit – finally, we got it straight and were able to haul the engine off onto the slip road. It turned out that our work on this day was appreciated: we had a letter of thanks from the Chief Motive Power Office of British Rail.

In November of the same year we were called out one night to Millom steel works. On arrival, we saw a shunt loco on its side and a wagon almost on top of it. The loco had been crossing over in the works when a raft of wagons ran into it sideways, knocking it over. The night was dark and moonless and the weather was atrocious. We could see that, because of the overhead pipes and steelwork, it would not be possible to use our steam crane, and jacking was going to be very difficult. I decided to take the bull by the horns and pull the wagon off the loco with the breakdown engine. And we had the most marvellous stroke of luck. As the wagon was being pulled away, its buffers caught on the loco, tipped it upright and – amazingly – dropped it straight back onto the track! All we had to do then was jack the wagon back onto the track.

The engine had very little damage and we were lucky to complete what should have been a long and awkward job in terrible weather, in such a short time. A week later a grateful letter of appreciation was sent by the manager of the steel works to my boss in Carnforth. After reading it, the boss said he was very pleased with us. But he never did know how we managed to get the job done so quickly.

We had some interesting and varied jobs requiring our breakdown unit, and one of these was at Barrow docks estate. The docks had their own 7-ton cranes which were used for unloading iron ore from wagons onto large heaps at the trackside. Usually, the ore came in shipments of large stones which could be picked up easily by the cranes' grabs. However, one shipload consisted of black powdered ore and the crane driver hadn't realised that a grab, full of powder, would weigh a lot more than the normal ore stone. As he had swung the crane round with this full grab, it tilted over and the whole crane ended up on its side, lying on a big heap of ore. We managed to heave it to a vertical position eventually, before the driver continued, this time taking a bit more care.

When I arrived at Barrow, I'd discovered that our own breakdown crane was one of the oldest in existence. It had no boiler, and got its steam power through a flexible pipe which had to be attached to a locomotive. It had just a 12' jib and a 15-ton lifting capacity, so was only really useful for putting wagons back onto the track. After I had been at the depot for about a year, a new crane was delivered to replace it. This one had its own power, a 47' jib and could lift 36 tons. This resulted in our being on call now for weekend work

The new 36-ton steam crane replaces the old 15-ton crane at Barrow depot in 1961.

lifting such things as bridges and girders, and it pleased the breakdown staff greatly because it meant extra money coming in for Sunday working and over-time.

One lunchtime, we had a derailment only about 40 yards from Barrow station. This kind of event always attracted a crowd of onlookers. We had almost finished re-railing the engine when I heard my name being called out from someone in the group of people behind the station fence. I walked over and found it was a fitter from my old depot at Wellingborough – Freddie Coles. He told me he had come to Vickers Armstrong shipyards for a course on diesel engines, which were being built at Barrow then. It was a real surprise and pleasure to see him because we had worked together at Wellingborough for over 20 years.

During my first 18 months at Barrow everything seemed to be happening at once and I was always on the go. One evening, when the wind was letting us all know we were on the north-west coast, I had a call from the depot to say that one of the main yard lights had gone out and drivers were having diffi-culty moving engines on the shed. I tried to contact the railway engineers' ODM (Outdoor Machinery) department but to no avail, so I rode down to the depot on my bicycle. The wind speed was about 50 to 60 mph and on the way there a powerful gust lifted my favourite trilby hat off my head and it sailed high in the air and away, never to be seen again.

When I arrived at the depot, I found that none of the staff were prepared to try to change the light bulb in those conditions, the light being at the top of a 40' pole reached by a vertical ladder. They all felt it was far too dangerous, so, because we really could not manage without the light, there was only one thing to do – and that was to do it myself. Although the pole was held by wire stays, I found that by the time I reached the top of the ladder it was swaying far too much for comfort. Somehow, I managed to hang on whilst changing the bulb before I started back down to solid ground. Once I'd reached the bottom of the ladder and the job was done, the brave lads who had been watching me were able to carry out their duties once again!

I settled in well at Barrow and, after I'd been there for about two years, I began to believe I knew enough about the job of shedmaster to get to the next grade. So I started applying for promotion again. I was called for an interview at a 'Special A' depot at Agecroft, Manchester. I had a terrible time. After about five minutes, the superintendent who interviewed me knew that I was not up to standard, and he really went to town, putting me through the worst half-hour of my life. He made me realise just how much I had to learn, and I felt so small when I left his office that I could have walked under the door without opening it! It taught me quite a sharp lesson and it was another 18 months before I dared to apply for promotion again.

As I bided my time, Vickers Armstrong were working hard on three big jobs. All three were completed before I left Barrow. The refit of the aircraft carrier *Hermes* was finished and the ship left the shipyard for tests on the open sea. More important was the completion of the nuclear submarine, *Dreadnought*. Both of these had to pass through a one-side lifting bridge on their way out, and to get *Hermes* through was a big operation. The ballast tanks had to be blown so that the vessel could lean over at an angle – an angle so acute that all the top deck was visible from the ground. As well as this, the whole lifting bridge was moved back several yards to give enough width for the ship to pass through the very narrow channel of water leading into the main docks. A big operation indeed.

The Queen came to launch the *Dreadnought* and also the third vessel to be completed, the new passenger liner, *Oriana*. It was a busy time for us because the Queen's special train had to run right into the shipyard and everything had to be just perfect. The engine, track, walkways and lighting all received careful attention. When all was ready Her Majesty duly arrived, and both events ran smoothly.

Soon, I braved another interview and this time I was better equipped. I was given the job of shedmaster at Stoke-on-Trent, famous for its potteries, so, after four happy years, the family had to say goodbye to the sea and the mountains and move back inland.

12 A shedmaster's job at Stoke-on-Trent

On my arrival in Stoke in 1961, finding somewhere to stay was difficult. Hotels were either too expensive, too crowded, or simply not up to scratch. After a week of trying different places, one of my foremen recommended a commercial hotel to me. I found it very clean, I had a nice bedroom and it wasn't too far from my work. For the first evening meal I was served stew and rice pudding, which was fine. It wasn't quite so enjoyable when the same meal arrived on the table the following evening, and the one after that, and the one after that. Indeed, after two months in the hotel, the residents had been served nothing but stew and rice pudding every single day! When I finally left the place to move into the house I'd bought for the family, I knew it would be a very long time before I fancied stew or rice pudding again.

My office at the depot was quite a nice one, originally having been built for the manager of the North Stafford Railway Company. It was about 25 feet square with a large desk, highly-polished brown linoleum and a huge coal fire.

With the breakdown crew on Stoke's 36-ton crane, 1962.

The staff numbered 665, including four foremen, a work-study officer and about 80 staff at Uttoxeter depot, for which I was also responsible. Here, there were 18 locos, whilst at Stoke our allocation was 75. We had Class 8 2-8-0 FRTs, five passenger 2-6-0 FRTs and four 0-6-0s, passenger tank locos and shunt engines.

The main line ran between the two engine sheds. One shed was very old, with its 3' thick walls forming the circular shape inside which was space for a dozen of the smaller locos. In the centre was a turntable. The other shed was straight-sided and much larger, housing about 24 locos. Of course, we had a breakdown train with its staff coach, a second holding all the jacking and packing equipment, and a 36-ton steam crane and match wagon. At the time I started work at Stoke-on-Trent, all the bridges in the area were being modified in preparation for the electrification of the main lines. Many weekends were spent with our crane being used for lifting off old bridges and replacing them with new ones.

The new bridges usually consisted of large concrete castings. These were manageable, as we knew the exact weight when setting the crane, but it was a different matter when it came to lifting off some of the quite ancient brick bridges. We found that the centres of these were often filled with rubble and pieces of old railway lines, making it almost impossible to gauge their correct weight. Consequently, we experienced many hair-raising moments, with the crane bouncing back and forth as we lifted an unknown quantity onto a wagon or trackside!

One evening, the engineers were working on the ironwork of an old bridge. They were removing bricks so that we could attach our steel ropes, when their acetylene cutter severed a hidden gas pipe. A sheet of flame, about 8 feet high, shot up from the rubble of the bridge, lighting up the night sky and affecting the supply of gas to the nearby village. It was some hours before the gas was shut off properly and we were able to resume work. However, it wasn't to be our lucky night....

I needed to reverse the crane to get to the other side of the bridge, which meant running 100 yards or so up to some points. I asked an engineer if there were any overhead wires in the area and he told me no, it was OK to make the move. So we moved. After travelling about 80 yards, our crane caught on an overhead power cable resulting in an immediate blackout of the whole village. It wasn't the villagers' lucky night either!

The longest weekend of all was spent in the Colwick area, where we'd been given two bridges to deal with instead of the usual one. We left Stoke depot at 9.00 p.m. on a Saturday, ready to work as quickly and efficiently as

(Above) preparing for electrification – a weekend job at Dudley Port in 1962, and (below) at Catchems Corner with Crewe's steam crane assisting.

possible. But this time our engineers ran into difficulties which took many hours to sort out, resulting in a long delay which saw us arriving back in Stoke at 7.00 a.m. on the Monday. We were absolutely shattered, but there was no point in complaining and gradually, we worked our way to the end of the list of bridge replacements.

During my early days at Stoke-on-Trent, work-study was becoming very important on the railways and I was sent on a course. It was held in the Taunton area, in a beautiful old mansion miles from the nearest town and a one-mile walk from the closest village. A few weeks previously we had introduced a work-study system into the shed at Stoke, and, about an hour before lunch one day, I happened to mention this to our course tutor. Oh, how I wished I'd kept my big mouth shut when his immediate reaction was, "Right – you can give us a talk on the work-study programme straight after lunch."

I could have dropped through the floor. I swallowed my lunch without tasting it while I wondered what on earth I could say. How would I even start? My only experience of this kind of thing had been in talking to small groups at meetings, when I was usually quite confident about my subject. Addressing a class of some 30 shedmasters and supervisors, at least half of whom were more highly-graded and far more experienced than me, was a different matter altogether.

But I had to do it, and somehow I got through the ordeal, helped by the proximity of a blackboard upon which I could sketch some of the procedures and talk at the same time without having to look at the class. I must have looked terrified and as white as a sheet, but no one said anything untoward and the course leader seemed reasonably pleased with my effort. I walked back to my chair, sank down in relief, and the course continued uneventfully for the remainder of the week.

Back at the depot, the breakdown train was in regular use as we had a fair number of derailments to deal with in the Stoke area. One of the most difficult occurred on the entrance to a triangle near Leek.

A single line led to the triangle, and, as it approached on this line, a Class 5 passenger FRT loco with three 27-ton wagons, was derailed. It was the coldest night of the year, about -12C, and the line was on a gradient of 1 in 45. In railway terms this is very steep. Because it was a single line, we couldn't get round the engine to reach the wagons behind it. All we could do was attach the crane onto the front of the loco itself. We began to lift the front end of the engine, but, although we took it very gently, it started to run towards us so we had to abandon that idea.

We decided to part the engine from the tender, although we knew we wouldn't be able to lift it completely because, even without a tender, it would still weigh about 50 tons. So we lifted the front of the engine high, putting packing material under the middle wheels. Then, we lowered the front end and swivelled the loco round, until the rear wheels were above the track. Lifting again, we removed the packing and lowered the loco onto the track.

After it was taken up to the triangle, we returned with the crane to lift the tender, which only weighed about 24 tons. Then, we did the same with the three 27-ton iron ore wagons.

Thinking we were almost there, we recoupled the engine to the tender, ready for taking away for repair and examination. We were all very cold and looking forward to getting home to a nice warm fire – but it wasn't to be. When we tried to move the breakdown vehicle, all its brakes had frozen solid and the whole thing started to skid. By the time we had loosened it up by carefully shunting it about, the operation had taken just over 24 hours.

This was 1963; a very hard winter when the temperature held at freezing point or below for about six weeks. In Stoke engine sheds we kept 76 large coal fires burning continuously in order to prevent the tank and water pipes on the engines from freezing. By now I had a telephone in the house, and one night, at 1.00 a.m., a call came through to say there was no water supply to the sheds; the locos were running short.

Our supply came from the canal which ran alongside the depot, and was fed from a 12" pipe which dipped under the water. Now, the canal was covered with solid ice, about 6" thick. The pipe left the canal and travelled about 12 to 15 yards above ground, and this length had frozen. The only thing to do was to build fires along the side of it, and wait. We were getting panicky calls; some from the loco sheds, to say that if there was no water soon then their fires would have to be knocked out; and some from our controllers who sat wondering in their warm offices. We waited with frozen feet for about four hours, and were finally rewarded with a loud gurgle from the end of the pipe where we had cut a hole in the ice. At last, water was getting through, but the first lot through the water columns on the shed was reported to be very muddy indeed!

On a far more pleasant winter morning, at about 7.30, a farmer was herding his sheep from a field on one side of the railway track to one on the opposite side. After getting all the animals out of the first field, he closed the gate behind him and crossed the rails to open the other one. This meant that, for a short while, the sheep were standing on or near the track. The railway line was a branch line at this point, a mile or so of completely straight rails, and just at this time one of my drivers with a large 2-8-0 FRT was travelling 'light engine' (no wagons or carriages attached) at about 50mph, towards the crossing place. Sadly, because he was driving directly into the strong glare of the rising sun, he didn't see the sheep until it was too late to stop in time. Twenty-six were killed or died from their injuries.

The matter went to the courts to determine who was ultimately responsible. My job was to estimate the braking distance of a 75-ton engine travelling at 50mph. This was very difficult because quite a lot depended on the state of the track at the time. It could well have been affected by dampness and the morning dew, which would result in the loco skidding, as only one inch of the wheel surface is in contact with the line at any one time. It's a long time ago now and I feel unsure of either the exact distance I gave the court (something like 120 yards) or, indeed, the final outcome of the case. But the driver could not really be blamed because of the conditions, and the fact that the sheep were left on the track between the closed gates.

13 Mechanical challenges and people problems

Gradually, the weather got warmer and spring turned to summer. And during that particular summer I had my first experience in the use of 'Kelbus Tackle'. Only the largest depots were issued with this equipment and Crewe breakdown team were fortunate to have it at theirs. One morning, a job came up that was going to need a lot of wood packing and a great deal of manual labour, and we'd been asked to help them. A Class 8 FRT 2-8-0 had run back through a set of catch points, coming off the track and finishing up at least 20 yards away in the soft earth of a grass field. The loco had travelled too far into the field to reach with a crane, and the ground was too soft for jacking.

It was a job for the Kelbus Tackle and, as we arrived, it was being taken out of the Crewe vans. It turned out to be just one massive pair of pulley blocks, each about 18" across and weighing over one hundredweight, the ropes being steel hawsers an inch thick. It was possible to fasten the tackle to the centre of the rail track and, with the efforts of a considerable number of workers, this was done. Then came the next heavy job.

We needed to build a path of 62 thick wooden blocks all the way from the catch points up to the engine in the field. This took a few hours and tons of packing from the Stoke and Crewe vans. When it was finished, a wire rope was fastened onto the loco, and the pulley block hook and pulling rope of the tackle were attached to the coupling hook of another engine. With this engine pulling on the steel ropes of the blocks, the loco was hauled slowly onto the wooden packing. The tackle had to be reset about four or five times before the derailed engine reached the catch points. After just a little readjustment, the engine climbed the points. The rest of it followed onto the rails until it was safely back on the main line. It was very muddy but had hardly any damage, having been re-railed by a very simple, but marvellously effective device.

On a summer morning, bright and early, I went with the breakdown crew to a derailment that had happened at Milton, near Stoke. It involved a Class 5 passenger FRT and a Class 8 FRT and brake van. Vandals had switched a set of points near a bridge where a line branched off the main line to a steel works. The action caused the engine to run off the rails in between two sets

Accident caused by vandals at Milton, Staffs, 1962. News cutting, Evening Sentinel.

of lines. Unfortunately, between these lines lay a 3' deep ditch. This resulted in the Class 8 being thrown off at an angle, before coming to a halt, causing the driver to be thrown against the hot steam pipes and suffer burns. To re-rail the engine and van proved very difficult, and we had to literally drag the engines back along their original paths before we could get them back on the rails. It took us almost a day.

But we did have a stroke of luck during the afternoon. British Railways (BR) police were mingling with the crowd of people watching from the bridge, when they overheard some lads boasting about how they'd altered the points. They were arrested promptly and charged with vandalism, which was quite a satisfactory outcome to us!

The gas board gave us a very interesting weekend job at Wednesbury. We had to place an 18" pipe, 137 feet long, onto brackets attached to the top of an aqueduct. The pipe had been laid along the track on trestles.

Our first task was to arrange the steel wire slings carefully, so that they wouldn't slip, and, at the same time, would hold the whole length of pipe firmly to prevent bowing. This done, we had to lift it up, turn it right round, and make it travel up to the aqueduct whilst being propelled by the breakdown engine. As it neared the brackets, I began to think we weren't going to be able to raise the pipe quite high enough. But eventually, with our 47 foot crane jib we just – and only just – managed it, without any damage to pipe or brackets. It had looked like a simple job, but was much more complex than it appeared.

So the jobs were challenging and varied, but there was also an interesting social side to work here. During every year of my four-year stay, a different engine driver happened be made Lord Mayor of Stoke-on-Trent. In addition, five were city councillors. Apart from one or two disagreements about time off for council matters, we all got on pretty well. This meant that my wife and I were invited to Lord Mayor's dinners, the Lord Mayor's Ball, and one lunch with the Mayor of Nuneaton. The Lord Mayor would invite a number of people he regarded as VIPs on outings, and we felt fortunate to be asked to visit potteries such as Wedgwood's where we could see the china-making process in action and make a purchase if something caught our eyes. Just before I left Stoke, we were looking forward to a visit to one of the nearby major coal mines, but it didn't happen. So many people argued with the Lord Mayor about who was going to be invited, that the outing had to be cancelled!

Talking of arguments, one winter a huge row blew up about the awarding or not of a gold watch. At that time, British Railways gave watches to employees who had completed 45 years service. A driver, who had been ill for some time, died within three days of his 45 years with the railway, and his wife asked if she could please have the watch, as it was so near the time. As I've said before, BR rules were rigid and she was told that she wasn't entitled to one.

The balloon went up! Within days it was reported in the national newspapers that an unfeeling British Railways had denied the poor widow her gold watch because of the three days. Wheels within BR started to turn very quickly then. Before the week was out a gold watch was sent to me from Crewe. This was accompanied by a phone call from my boss, along the lines of: "Get out now and deliver the watch personally to the driver's wife – and apologise on behalf of British Railways". This was at 6.00 p.m. on a cold and foggy night.

In industrial Stoke-on-Trent, the fog always came down like a thick, wet blanket and we had some real 'pea-soupers'. On this occasion visibility was too poor for me to go by car, so I decided to cycle. The city, with its six towns, was a big one and stretched in all directions. The driver had lived on a new estate that I had never even heard of and to find it on a foggy night was some job. It must have been about four miles from my house, and I finally arrived at my destination two hours later, having stopped to ask directions many times over.

When I entered the widow's house my troubles really started. The whole family had assembled there to wait for me and, for the next half hour, I was subjected to a veritable ear bashing about the stinginess and other faults of British Railways. I tried to defend myself and the depot by explaining that I didn't make the rules, but of course it made no difference. The only thing to do was to sit and bite my tongue to save us from even more trouble! Needless to say, I wasn't offered a nice hot drink after my cold journey, but eventually I made my escape and got back on my bike. After another hour and a half I arrived home; after a hard day's work and a harder evening, the warmth of home was very welcome and it was a great relief to fall into bed.

The discussions that evening had been difficult, and the fact that I didn't always understand the local accent had made it worse. As well as speaking with a strong North Staffordshire brogue, people threw in lots of local words which I had to try to remember. So, on a cold day, someone like my mechanical foreman, who was an excellent man, would say it was 'nesh'.

Not long before I was due to leave Stoke, this foreman was walking round one of the sheds when he came across a fitter who was apparently having difficulty in removing a bottom slidebar from a Class 8 engine. He went over to the man and said, "Come on, let me have a go." He picked up the crowbar and gave it a good heave. This caused the slidebar, which weighed over a hundredweight and had very sharp edges, to suddenly come loose and drop onto his feet, cutting off one of his big toes. After three months' sick leave he came back, leaning on a stick and having difficulty maintaining his balance. Accidents were all too common in those days.

One very useful benefit of my promotion to Stoke was my new entitlement to first class travel on British Railways for both me and my wife. This was very handy, especially during the more popular holiday times. Our busiest time was 'Wakes Week' which fell at the end of July. It was the potteries' main holiday, when nearly all of Stoke went all over the country from Blackpool to Yarmouth. On the first weekend we had 25 extra engines drafted in to us, mostly Class 5 passenger FRT locos. The depot was chock-a-block with engines from Friday and trains started leaving Stoke station from around 3.00 a.m. on Saturday. It was an all-night job for me, trying to ensure that everything was ready and running to time on our most important day of the year.

As well as organising the work in Stoke-on-Trent, I had to keep an eye on things in Uttoxeter. On one of my visits there I came across a tiny, battery-driven loco with a central driving cab. Probably, it had been used for shunting in one of the local marshalling yards. Now it was in rather poor condition; dirty grey with its number, BEL2, and a BR sign on its side just

Battery-operated shunting loco at Uttoxeter, 1964.

visible through the grime. Some 20 years later, I came across this same little loco again, now resplendent in maroon and white livery and residing at York Railway Museum. The words 'North Stafford Railway' had been painted onto its sides, along with the original North Staffordshire emblem: the Staffordshire knot. It was so good to see it with a new lease of life!

I had been in Stoke for almost four years when a position was advertised in Liverpool. This was a higher-graded job and I managed to get an interview at the divisional office there. I thought it went quite well, but I wasn't offered the job. Only a month later, the shedmaster's job at Birkenhead became vacant and I had another interview with the same people. It was very short and I thought to myself, "Well, that was a waste of time – all that way for a 10-minute interview!"

Three weeks later, I had the surprise of my life when a letter arrived telling me the job was mine; I realised then that my first interview had been taken into account and there wasn't all that much to cover the second time. So, it was goodbye to smoky Stoke (as it was then!) and hello to Birkenhead; a place I'd hardly heard of until it came up for selection on our vacancy list.

14 An office by the Mersey: starting at Birkenhead

When I arrived in Birkenhead in May 1965 I found lodgings in Prenton, near Tranmere football ground. My landlord was an ex-shipyard boilermaker so with my father being a boilersmith, the two of us found plenty to talk about. I stayed with him for four months, until we sold the house in Stoke and managed to find another in the more costly region of the Wirral.

During these months in Prenton I tried to find out all about the area I'd come to. In the evenings I used to catch a Mersey Rail electric train to one of the stations on the line and then walk back via the road or the beach. This way I covered all the stations between Birkenhead, New Brighton and West Kirby. One of our divisional driving inspectors turned out to be someone I knew who'd worked at Rugby back in my Market Harborough days. Now, he was very helpful to me, showing me all round the Wirral marshalling yards and sidings. He lived by the sea at West Kirby, a very attractive place with open areas of National Trust land, a long promenade and a marine lake.

All this and only 25 minutes by train to Birkenhead – I decided I liked this town very much and it wasn't too long before I found a house here. We settled down happily. The Mersey area was all very interesting to me, whether it was travelling under the river by train or paying four pence to cross it on the ferry. The ferry boat gave you a really good view of all the boats going in and out of the docks. The biggest ship I ever saw was the Japanese oil tanker, *MARU*, which looked absolutely massive. At 100 yards long and weighing over 250,000 tons, it dwarfed everything around it. One of my Mersey line cleaners told me that, in the middle of the night, when the tunnel was quiet, the propellers of these great ships could be heard quite distinctly as they passed overhead on their way down the river.

On either side of the River Mersey there was a huge pump. I saw them once, these great machines which pumped out the tunnel running beneath the main railway tunnels. This lower tunnel absorbed all the seepage which came through the rocks. It was inspected constantly by boat and the water was pumped out at a continuous rate of 25,000 gallons an hour. During the war, bombs dropped in and around the Mersey had increased the seepage considerably over pre-war levels and it was said that, if the pumps were to stop, the rail tunnels would be flooded within three hours.

At night the lights of the Liverpool waterfront made a wonderful sight as I gazed on them from the Birkenhead side of the river. The Liver Building, the Anglican cathedral and the revolving tower restaurant were all floodlit. Lights shone from all the big office windows and waterfront street lamps and I grew to love this view.

I had to familiarise myself with all the Birkenhead docks and railway yards which, at that time, stretched from Bidston to Birkenhead – a distance of several miles. At Bidston yard and sidings, all the iron ore was loaded into the John Summers steelworks wagons, ready to be hauled the 12 miles to the works near Chester. As well as iron ore and steel, we dealt with all manner of goods: coal, china clay, old bones, fishmeal and cattle. This was 1965, and a very busy time for us. We had sixteen 350hp diesel shunt locos working in the marshalling yards at Morpeth, Bidston and Birkenhead.

The entrance to Birkenhead motive power depot was reached via Mollington Street, a short little road where eight tiny two-up, two-down terraced houses stood along one side. In those days we all had coal fires and I began to wonder why a coal lorry never visited this street. The reason soon became apparent when one day, when I was walking along a siding on the edge of the depot, I walked straight into a little boy. He was about six or seven years old and was just about able to stagger along with the large lump of coal he was carrying. When he saw me he dropped the coal and dived straight under a large Class 8 FRT locomotive. The engine was in steam and could have moved off at any time but, when I got round to the other side, he had gone – no doubt back to his family who were waiting to stoke up the living room fire! One family in this little street had no less than 10 children, aged from one to 14. How they managed to live in such conditions I don't know, but all the youngsters looked very healthy and strong.

Birkenhead was mainly a freight depot, serving steelworks, docks and coal merchants, and running trains to Crewe and Chester with a lot of oil traffic from the large refinery at Ellesmere Port. We had 60 Class 9 2-10-0 FRT locos and 30 others consisting of Class 8 FRTs, Class 4 FRTs, Class 3 passenger tanks and shunt locos. There were two big engine sheds which would each hold about 20 locos; a workshop; a clothing store and main material and parts store; coaling plants and ash plants. Footplate staff; technical staff; shed and office staff; five train crew supervisors; a mechanical foreman and a foreman cleaner made a total of 525 people. The footplate staff covered the working of both the steam locos and the Mersey electric trains.

Locos on Birkenhead shed, 1963. Photo N. K. Harrop.

In my early days at the depot I had a lot of help from my Senior Traincrew Supervisor, a Welshman named Edwin Owen. He had a great deal of experience with staff and had, it was said, the ability to charm the birds off the trees. His talent lay in staff relations and he was enormously encouraging to me, helping me to get to know what to expect from the quick-witted Merseyside character! Sixty-five staff in the sheds were engine cleaners, all aged between 18 and 25 and a very spirited bunch of lads. Some 20 or 30 of these could be working on the shed at the same time and the foreman cleaner had his work cut out in keeping them under control. They'd get up to all sorts of tricks; some simply for fun and others to get out of doing any work. Now and again we'd have the odd fight breaking out or a few broken windows to investigate, so there was never a dull moment where they were concerned!

Every year, each driver and passed fireman was interviewed to make sure they were in receipt of all the pages in the rule book and amendments to working and so on. Then they would sign a register to that effect. It was a tedious job for the train crew supervisor, who had to see at least 300 men who were on all manner of shifts, off sick or on holiday. But it was essential to know that each man was aware of current regulations. Another huge task was the compilation of driver rosters for winter and summer workings and Bank Holidays. The final lists had to have the agreement of the staff and, as it often resulted in disagreements, would generally take a week or so.

The chairman of the staff side at the motive power depot was Jack Johnson. He was a very dedicated railwayman who worked hard at every meeting to get the best deal he possibly could for the footplate staff. He was a highly intelligent man who excelled in his job and had a detailed knowledge of all rules and regulations. He was also a very persistent man who pursued all staff complaints vigorously, making my life a very busy one! Absolutely dedicated to his union and the needs of the staff, he had a great sense of fairness and could always see the management's position along with his own. Jack was a good friend outside work and I was pleased and not surprised to see him finish his working life as the area union representative for the whole of the northwest district of British Rail.

We had some colourful characters on the staff at Birkenhead. One day, I arrived at work and realised that I'd forgotten the key to the Yale lock on my office door. I thought there was nothing for it but to send someone back to West Kirby to fetch it for me – but I was wrong. One of the shed staff had realised my predicament and offered to help. This wiry little man said he could open the door for me so I asked him, "Have you got a key then?" "No," he replied, "but I won't be a minute." He wouldn't let me go to the office with him, but was back in two or three minutes, telling me proudly, "OK – it's open."

I walked along to my office. The door was open; the Yale lock was fastened open; there was no sign of forced entry. It certainly made me wonder what kind of work he'd been doing before he joined the railway!

All footplate staff were issued with a uniform; a hat, jacket and trousers which were replaced every three years. Some people wore them out in no time at all, while others were more careful of their clothes and made them last for years. One day, a driver, looking very frightened, turned up at the depot in the company of a civilian policeman. This officer was concerned because he had witnessed the man trying to sell a considerable number of railway overalls and jackets that he had obviously accumulated.

Although British Railways was strict about many things, when it came to clothing, a driver could do exactly what he liked with his uniform issue as long as he came properly dressed for duty. It took me quite a while to convince the policeman that this was indeed the case. This particular driver, a senior man, must have been saving up his unused clothing for years until he felt he had enough to sell for a bit of extra money. The policeman was finally persuaded all was above board, although he wasn't very pleased with the situation. The driver, meanwhile, was a distinctly relieved man because any staff convicted of stealing were dismissed instantly.

15 Steam power ends in a huge explosion

The year 1967 was a time of big changes on the railways. The old position of District Motive Power Superintendent was dispensed with and area managers began to take charge of all footplate staff, sheds, marshalling yards, stations and signal boxes. The technical side was placed under newly-created Maintenance Engineers.

We were very busy at Birkenhead depot at that time, using 3,000,000 gallons of water and 2,000 tons of coal in a year. Dieselisation and electrification of the main lines was fast approaching, and many weekends saw us out with the 36-ton crane, lifting out stone bridges and replacing them with new square-topped constructions of concrete and steel. Signal posts also had to be replaced. We even took on the lifting in of concrete beams for the reconstruction of Birmingham New Street station. These were very tiring times because, after a long weekend spent working in all kinds of weather, we were of course still expected to carry out the next week's work as normal. This was a bit of a job, especially if we'd only arrived back at the depot in the early hours of Monday morning.

In 1968 the area manager's operating assistant at Morpeth dock retired. After a talk with my area manager, somehow I'd managed to convince him that I could do this job as well as my own. The new post of Assistant Area Manager, Movements was created. This meant promotion for me, and by the time I'd taken on two extra marshalling yards, shunters, number takers, dockers, a yard master and six inspectors, my staff total had risen to around 700. Needless to say, it was quite a responsibility to take on and my days were busier than ever. Soon after I took up my new position, along came a new area manager who turned out to be a very different cup of tea from the previous man. Every morning, at 10.00 a.m. prompt, I had to attend a meeting in his office. Here, he proceeded to unload as much work as possible onto the other assistant and myself. When he'd finished we carried heaps of papers; his desk was empty and he could sit back and enjoy the rest of the day.

On the operating side of my job, I had to keep up good relations with 24 dockers who seemed determined to make life difficult. They knew every trick in the book to ensure that they either stopped work or got extra money on a regular basis. For instance, 'unloading goods in the rain' nearly always meant a bit more cash in their pockets. In addition, the guards who were domiciled at Morpeth docks were led by two or three militants who would frequently stop work at the drop of a hat. So I certainly had to keep on top of things.

The staff at the depot were a really mixed bunch, consisting of ex-Western, ex-Central and ex-Midland railwaymen along with quite a number who had transferred to Birkenhead because of shortage of work at their own depot or for promotion. As Wales was not far away, over the years we had many transfers from that direction; in fact so many that at one time we had 22 staff named Williams and 16 by the name of Jones. This caused a bit of confusion at times because quite a few had the same initials and there were two or three sets of brothers. So we had to manage by identifying them by various titles such as Communist Jack, Brombrough Jack, Donkey Jones, John 1, John 2, JB and so on...

I admit freely that most of the above were quite a handful to manage. They were streetwise, sharp and quick to take advantage of any mistakes made, and I had to keep my eyes wide open. They'd come up with all kinds of reasons to get a day off work. I remember one occasion very clearly. A driver, sad expression etched on his face, came into my office and asked for leave to bury his grandmother. Fortunately, we kept careful records and, on checking these, I found he'd used this excuse before and told him so very sharply. He thought about this, and, with no sign of embarrassment at all said, "Sorry boss – I couldn't have been thinking straight." Off he went, as cool as a cucumber. And many of the others would have done the same! I have to say though, that, colourful as they were, they were a very warm-hearted bunch and quick to help anyone in trouble, and I soon realised that they would be more generous with their money and support than any staff at my previous depots.

By now Birkenhead was one of the last motive power depots retaining steam locomotives – locomotives which would soon be gone for ever. One of our most important responsibilities was the conveyance of iron ore from Bidston dock to John Summers' steelworks at Shotton, near Chester. We ran 12 trains daily, each one having eleven 88-ton wagons loaded with ore, and one brake van. The total concentrated train weight was 1,000 tons. The locomotive pulling this was the largest type on British Railways; a Class 9 2-10-0, weighing over 80 tons itself when loaded with coal and water.

The main working problem with these particular trains was that firstly, after leaving Bidston, there was a steady uphill gradient for about six miles. So on this stretch of line the engines were working hard. Secondly, and more dangerous, was a downhill run of nearly eight miles into John Summers' sidings at Shotton. This meant that 1,080 tons had to be controlled down the hill. I travelled with this train several times and it was quite unsettling to feel the huge weight pushing at us behind the engine.

To keep control of these trains the driver and guard needed to have a great deal of experience coupled with sound local knowledge, especially in wet weather when the braking was affected by slippery rails. The guard kept his brake on all the time and the driver had also to apply a steady and controlling pressure on his brakes. This was necessary because, as well as having to turn from main line into siding, he had to be prepared to stop at a signal before the entrance of the siding in order to cross over the adjacent main line. On arrival at Shotton the brake blocks would frequently be almost red hot or, at the least, would have turned blue with the heat.

Finally, the big day came when the last steam train would run from Bidston to Shotton. Sir Richard Summers, boss of this huge steelworks, was a big fan of British Rail and it was decided that he would drive this train on its final trip. We sorted out a uniform and cap for the purpose and, under the strict supervision of a district inspector, off he went. It was a momentous occasion, plenty of people turning out to watch. Sir Richard enjoyed himself immensely on the footplate of a Class 9 locomotive, was photographed for the local paper, and drove the train into the steelworks safely with its final load.

After steam had gone these trains were hauled by 2750hp Sultzer diesel locos which, whilst they had a good resource of power to climb the gradient out of Bidston, still needed a lot of care and attention to keep the trains under proper control when running towards Shotton.

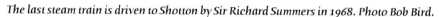

The last steam train is driven to Shotton by Sir Richard Summers in 1968. Photo Bob Bird.

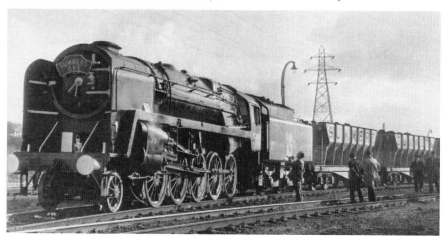

The engine they could not save, 42942, on one of its last outings as a passenger train in 1966.

It was 1969 and the new diesel fuelling plant had been completed. The time had come for all steam stock to be either sent away or put in store in our sidings. One of these locos, a 2-6-0 Crab Class 5 mixed traffic engine, was the last of its kind to be in full working order and was very popular with railway enthusiasts. A local society was formed with the aim of raising £2,500, the sum required by BR for the purchase of this engine. Pamphlets were circulated and photographs were printed in the local newspaper, and the depot had many visits from people just wanting to have what could be a last look at 42942. I think the engine was so admired because of its versatility. It had good-sized wheels and enough power to make it strong enough for pulling a freight train and fast enough for passenger train working – a real work-horse for the railway. But, despite their best efforts, the members of the society failed to raise the money in time. Like so many others, the engine was taken away to be cut up.

During this time we had quite a lot of trouble with thefts of brass and copper from the stored locos. The steel was also of very high quality and much sought-after by scrap merchants. In fact one day, a scrap merchant came to see me and offered to pay me £5 for the pistons from a loco. I had no authority to sell this material, which was worth at least ten times the amount he offered me, and soon saw him off the premises.

Now that dieselisation was complete we needed no more coal and ashes on the depot, and only small quantities of water. So we had a good clean-up of the shed and cleared away all the heaps of fuel and ashes, making the depot a cleaner and tidier place to work. Some months later it was arranged that the ash and coaling plants would be demolished. A very colourful character nick-named 'Blaster Bates' was employed to do the job. Blaster, real name Derek Macintosh Bates, had been a bomber pilot during the war and then became a bomb disposal expert. At the end of World War II, his knowledge of explosives spurred him on to start his own business as a demolition specialist. He would explode anything from chimneys to septic tanks and, in later years, Mr Bates was a popular after-dinner speaker who kept his audience entertained with tales of his exploits. He appeared a number of times on television and his stories were made into sound recordings.

On this occasion the explosion was arranged for a Sunday morning. When demolition day came, for some reason, known only to himself, Blaster Bates made his entrance at the depot wearing the almost complete uniform of a German soldier!

All wagons and engines were taken as far away from the plants as possible. While this was happening, Blaster was setting up his explosives which had to be placed with great care so that all the plants would fall lengthways and not across the tracks – which would have brought all movement on the depot to a halt! Everything was ready by 12 noon but we were unable to go ahead because of all the sightseers. Half the population of Birkenhead must have heard about it and people were coming from all directions to see the demolition take place. It took almost an hour to move the crowds to a safe distance.

Finally, at about 1 p.m. the button was pressed. The ash plants went first,

The steam age disappears: demolition of the coal hopper in 1968. News cutting: Liverpool Echo

two sharp cracks in the front legs being followed almost immediately by two in the back legs. Down they came, right along the ash pits as planned. The demolition of the coaling plant was a very impressive sight indeed. It was a massive building, about 100 feet tall and containing heavy machinery. After four booming explosions it started to fall, very gently at first, but then followed by a tremendous rushing sound and an enormous thud which shook the ground all over the depot. It left a thick pall of coal dust that cleared the area of people much quicker than we had been able to! It fell alongside the tracks, leaving us a massive clearing-up operation which took us some weeks to finish. Whether Blaster added the job to his store of tales I don't know – nothing had gone wrong and it was probably too straightforward to make much of a story. But it was another significant day in the disappearance of steam locomotion.

16 Busier than ever and a final promotion

Over the previous year we had introduced a big training programme for all our drivers; the technical staff also had been retrained to deal with the new type of power, and by now we were virtually ready for action. British Railways had been rebranded as British Rail to mark the fundamental change in the system. And a huge change it was for all of us who were brought up with steam, but such a busy time that there was little of it to spend in reminiscence!

During the changeover, everything went well apart from the fact that we'd only received about half the number of diesels expected. Although we managed, it was a real struggle to cover all our train work at first.

One of the first, and very special, jobs we had to arrange using the new power was the transportation of a nuclear reactor for a submarine. It was to be carried on a train travelling out of the docks and on to Cammel Lairds' works. The journey took place at 2.00 a.m. one morning and, with the aid of a 350hp shunt engine, we began the journey at walking pace.

The whole train was wired from end to end with alarm bells. These were to warn us of any signs the reactor might show of 'going wild'. Police and firemen were stationed along every part of the track and the whole experience felt rather weird and disquieting. The last 100 yards or so ran down a steep incline and to have a runaway train of this nature would have been a disaster. But it pulled into the works safe and sound and I was very glad that it was all over without a hitch.

Now that we were fully dieselised we had another problem to solve and this was to find an alternative locomotive to use under the River Mersey. Until now, if any of the Mersey Rail electric trains failed, a steam shunt loco could be sent in to handle the emergency and haul out the train and passengers to a station or to the repair depot at Birkenhead North. This would also be done in the event of a complete power failure. Now we were without steam we had to test alternatives.

So one morning at 2.00 found me under the Mersey on a Type 4 Brush-Sultzer diesel locomotive. We had to run through all the tunnels to see if it would be suitable. It turned out to be a bit of a nightmare as the extra height

One of the old Wirral engines, 1923.

and the 60' length of the engine proved to be very hazardous when negotiating the fairly sharp bends in the tunnels. When the Mersey railway first opened in 1886, steam engines were used to pull coaches of passengers from Liverpool under the river and on to the Wirral, and the tunnel walls were still black from all the smoke that couldn't escape. As we travelled through, I thought what a smelly and smoky time those first passengers must have had until the train climbed out of the tunnel. The top of our cab was only missing these walls by a few inches and we couldn't afford to get stuck under the river!

This type of loco, then, was not suitable for the work and we had to think again. After a fair bit of consideration, we ordered a special battery-powered coach which could not only do the job but would also help us with any night-time repair work needed in the tunnels. As it happened, the coach was never needed during the rest of my time at Birkenhead but it was always available with its huge number of batteries, should it ever become necessary to utilise it.

From 1969 I became busier and busier. Retraining for diesels, alterations for stores and equipment meant meeting after meeting. Many of these were to set up local agreements at Birkenhead, but a lot more took place at depots and places where our drivers had to work the trains. New train loading regulations came into force and it took many months of negotiations with staff to hammer out the final agreement.

I was now fully responsible for arranging and chairing all meetings with the operating, technical and shed staff and couldn't afford to make any mistakes. The staff side representatives were right there 'on the ball' and it was easy for them to keep in touch with colleagues anywhere on British Rail through our internal phone system. Occasionally, this meant they were in possession of information before management had even heard of it. So I spent many hours both at home and at work preparing for these meetings, hoping that I could get agreements pushed through which would suit my divisional managers. Any mistakes would result in unintended things slipping through, and news racing along the railway grapevines along the lines of 'Birkenhead's got it, so we want it!' With very similar speed my bosses would also get to know and I'd be in deep trouble.

Every 12 months or so, we had a visit from a group of inspectors. The Mechanical Inspector came to make sure we were doing our job properly by keeping up-to-date records of the mechanical side of things: engine examinations, tools and so on. The Fire Inspector came to ensure we had regular checks on the fire extinguishers and recorded them carefully; and the Auditors came to check the accuracy of all our office records. Naturally, they were keen to show that they were doing their own jobs properly and were very eagle-eyed when looking for faults.

One year, after giving us a good going-over, the only discrepancy one auditor could find was in our postage stamp record book. An entry read 'Jack owes one'. One of the clerks had borrowed a stamp for a personal letter, fully intending to replace it later. The fuss the auditor caused about this was almost unbelievable. I stood with the office staff as he ranted and raved about keeping accurate records and the abuse of company possessions. After insisting on our word that we would never do anything like this again, he calmed down; he had done his job.

The constant pressure of the last few years was beginning to affect my health. Whilst I was working at Stoke-on-Trent I had started to develop a stomach ulcer. Now, with my hefty workload, it was really playing up. I became quite ill and was sent into Hoylake hospital for two weeks' complete rest. This actually did me a lot of good and I went back to work, ready to tackle the latest set of problems.

Soon afterwards, in 1972, we had another 'rationalisation'. This cut out the Morpeth Dock area manager and the yard was now under management from Birkenhead. I was promoted to Train Crew Manager and now all the guards in the Wirral area joined my staff. The work and the meetings increased.

This was a time of frequent industrial disputes in the Liverpool and Birkenhead docks areas and the handling of cargo coming in and out of the ports was seriously affected. It seemed to me to be the beginning of a decline in the use of the ports, and the number of ships coming into the Mersey dropped considerably. Within a year or two, some of the large firms such as Tate & Lyle had pulled out of Liverpool, causing us to close Bidston marshalling yard. Oil tankers still came in for Ellesmere Port refinery, but this was the only business still needing substantial rail traffic. The reduction of the marshalling of wagons meant that yard staff had to be cut along with shunt locos, and the result was a considerable number of angry and highly-charged meetings with staff representatives.

Meanwhile, British Rail raced along in its quest for re-organisation. In 1974 the whole of the Wirral was placed under one area manager who had to have two associates: an Operations Manager and a Passenger Manager. These positions were a grade higher than my own and, although I was 56 years old, I thought I'd have one last try for promotion. I applied for the post of Operations Manager.

Because my experience of the operations side of work was somewhat limited, I really did think that I stood very little chance of getting this job. However, I got onto the short list and had a nerve-wracking interview which went about half as well as I would have liked it to. I put it out of my mind; seven of the other applicants were senior to me in grade service and had the right experience.

Two weeks later I had the shock of my life when my boss rang me and told me the job was mine. I could hardly take it in and this phone call was followed by quite a few sleepless nights. Could I do the job and make a success of it? The position meant responsibility for 823 staff who ranged from inspectors to signalmen and everyone else besides. I'd just have to try and stay positive and trust in myself.

17 A couple of bombshells and the computer arrives

After nine years in the same office at Mollington Street, I prepared to move out. I'd become very accustomed to the staff here over these years and they couldn't have thought I'd been too bad because they gave me a very nice send-off. I was touched to receive a gold Parker pen and pencil and, for my wife Kath, six crystal sherry glasses.

The following Monday, I moved into my new office at Birkenhead Central Station. I was just settling myself in when the door opened and my boss walked in. "I'm off to another job on Monday," he said, "and as senior assistant you'll be the one in charge."

So off he went, after I'd been there just a week. He'd been promoted to a higher position in London, leaving me as Acting Area Manager. This was three grades above the job I'd been in just a week ago, and to say I was as nervous as a kitten was an understatement! I was overwhelmed by the speed of events and it took me a while to realise what had happened to me in such a short time.

I buckled down and got on with it. But, just as I was beginning to get used to the idea, another bombshell dropped. Every year or so, area managers were visited by the 'top brass' from BR headquarters. They required a précis which gave an overall picture of the area; which meant a work of at least 30 pages. It would show everything from unit costs to staff costs; all the workings of the yards and depots; the freight and passenger train workings – in fact, all that went on at Birkenhead. I had about two weeks' notice to produce this document, which had to be copied 20 times to all concerned in our divisional office. Fortunately, I found a copy of the previous year's précis which gave me a good idea of what was needed. For the next two weeks I worked more than 12 hours a day, digging out all the current information and trying to get it all down on paper.

The day of the visit arrived all too soon and along came six officers, all specialists in their own field of work. They'd travelled in a special coach fitted with large windows, armchairs and a new kitchen. An attendant, smart in his uniform, waited on them. The Operating Manager (a man ranked two or three grades above me) and I, along with our local managers, were asked to step into the coach whereupon we were taken on a tour of our area. As we travelled to every yard, dock, siding and depot we were questioned in turn about the running of everything from signalboxes to stations, and the use of wagons and locomotives. The trip lasted about two hours and my nerves were in shreds, but I managed to struggle through it all without incident – much to the relief of our own managers. My relief when I got off that coach was something marvellous and that night I had my first decent night's sleep in weeks!

I covered the area manager's job for two months and it was a very hectic time of meetings, presentations and various visits. But eventually, the new man arrived to fill the post and, finally, I was able to settle down into my new job. I had so much to learn and over 800 staff in all kinds of work to get to know. Things were relatively quiet for six months and then we faced a major new challenge. British Rail was becoming computerised!

A main computer had been set up at Marylebone in London and every area manager's office was fitted with a computer to feed information back to it. Ours was situated in my room. I was sent to Woking on a two weeks' crash course to learn how to use the machine and master all the different codes for the types of information we'd be entering. On one particular Sunday, the system was set up. Details of all the wagons and rolling stock on British Rail were fed into the Marylebone computer, giving the type, number and stabling location.

From now on, every day we had to enter the numbers and position of every wagon and coach in our area. So, in order to find any wagon on BR all we should have to do was tap in the current code and the exact position would be revealed. As you can imagine, it was fun at first. With inexperienced hands sometimes tapping out the wrong code on the keys, reams of paper would pour out – unstoppable until someone rang Marylebone to cancel it.

Once set up though, this system saved British Rail from having to employ the hundreds of number-takers who toured the marshalling yards and sidings collecting wagon numbers. Almost all these men were absorbed into other work such as shunting or guard duties. Every morning my desk was covered in sheets of computer paper giving the whereabouts of our own rolling stock as well as that of other areas. We were always short of cattle wagons, but now we could search and find some and then ask the depots concerned to release them for our use at Birkenhead. Eventually, all locomotives were added to the system, along with their examination details, so that we could make better use of their availability.

There was a lot of oil traffic to deal with from the refineries at Ellesmere Port, most of the trains being made up of 100-ton rail tankers. Each train was

Bowler-hatted but still on a breakdown! Two diesels collide at Birkenhead in 1975. Photo Bob Bird.

very big and heavily loaded with many tons of oil, so it was quite a job to re-rail them after an accident. Apart from their weight and length being a problem, the bogie wheels always seemed to have minds of their own when we tried to put them back on the track.

One foggy morning, at about six o'clock, we had a bad derailment on the main line running through Birkenhead docks, blocking all movement in and out of the dock estate. Two 2750hp diesels had collided head-on at a speed of about 15mph. An error of yard control had allowed one loco to enter the dock before the other had left it. Fortunately both drivers had jumped clear before the impact and were unhurt.

This turned out to be one of our most difficult re-railing operations. One diesel, with its driver's cab almost squashed flat, was badly damaged and seemed to be trying to climb over the other. We managed to part the locos without too much trouble by tying one down to the rails, and giving the other a good tug with another hefty diesel. The first one was back on the track in good time and was towed away to the depot for examination, but the other loco's front bogie was so badly damaged that the wheels just wouldn't stay on the track. The only way to deal with it was to jack up the whole front end so that we could hold the bogie clear of the rails to enable us to haul it into a siding. Here, it could be made safe enough to travel to the main works for repair but it took many hours to get to this stage.

Just as important as making things safe was keeping things clean, and the cleanliness of diesel multiple unit carriages and Mersey Rail stock came under my supervision. Apart from graffiti on the inside of the carriages, one of our most awkward jobs was the removal of all the chewing gum left and trodden into the carriage floors by the hundreds of children who travelled to and from school. The cleaners would use cleaning fluid and a scraper but it wasn't very successful and would take hours to clean just one coach. But after a good bit of research we discovered the existence of a spray canister which revolutionised the process! One squirt and the gum froze solid, so that it could be removed quite easily in a fraction of the time. A seemingly small item like this made a huge difference to staff time and, consequently, cleaning costs.

Passengers used to leave all kinds of things on the trains, especially hats, macs and umbrellas. Strangely, the favourite items seemed to be walking sticks. We had a large bundle of these, some of them very nicely finished with silver or bone handles. But having so many always made me wonder: Why did a person need a stick when they got on the train, but not when they got off?

During the winter months, it was my responsibility to decide whether or not it was necessary to call out the 'Frost Train' for use on the third rail on the Mersey electric lines between Birkenhead, New Brighton and West Kirby. The electric trains were powered by flat metal slippers, about a yard long and riding on this 6500-volt third rail. In normal circumstances this worked perfectly well, but ice and snow caused severe shorting and flashing, resulting in loss of power and delays to this important passenger service. The frost train sprayed a special solution onto the rails to prevent them from freezing. It had to be worked at night and so it was an expensive exercise. I had to judge the weather very carefully. If the expected frost didn't materialise, then the train had been called out for nothing; if frost or snow came upon us unexpectedly, then the trains would be slipping about all over the place and I'd be in trouble with my superiors. Thank goodness I managed to get it right most of the time – although I do recall one particularly bad morning when we had a severe hailstorm which clogged up the slipper on a train and caused quite a few delays.

18 Adapting to retirement and pedal-power

In 1976 I went into Broad Green hospital at Birkenhead. I had to have my gall bladder removed and the result was an absence from work of almost four months. It was a long time to be away from my job and there was a great deal of catching up to do along with the usual round of meeting after meeting. There was extra pressure from training courses in Crewe and Woking, each lasting three to four weeks with working days that started at 8.30 a.m. and finishing at 10.00 p.m. The industrial relations side of my work was becoming more and more complex; now I had six different local departmental committees I met with regularly to thrash out problems. Most of my weekends were taken up with trying to catch up with all the paperwork it all produced.

I was becoming both mentally and physically exhausted. My ulcer was

My retirement presentation, with my wife Kath and the acting Area Manager on 30th June, 1978. Photo Bob Bird

playing up and I had difficulty sleeping. Now and then, I'd have to have some time off work to try and get fit for duty again. It may be hard to believe, but despite all this I still really enjoyed my work. However, in 1978, the constant pressure led me to decide that something needed to be done.

I met with my superiors for a long discussion. It was decided that, after 46 years of service on the railways, I would retire in June on grounds of ill-health. I didn't want to go. This had been my life for so many years, but I knew my health would have got worse and so I felt I had no choice.

Leaving was a very big wrench for me but the staff gave me a great send-off and I still treasure some very special gifts. And within two or three months of leaving I began to feel very much fitter. On daily four or five-mile walks I began to rediscover the beauty of the area I lived in. I walked to the islands off the coast and watched seals basking and all the comings and goings of a great variety of seabirds. (And of course, as I continued to improve I was able to catch up with all the jobs waiting for me in the house and garden!)

The following year I joined the Railway Superannuants' Club at Chester. We met once a month here and it was certainly a place for reunions. I met up again with my old chief clerk from Stoke-on-Trent and the shedmaster I had replaced at Barrow. There was plenty to talk about aside from the interesting speakers arranged. The meetings were well attended and I frequently landed myself with the job of making at least 80 cups of coffee. In the summer, outings were organised and wives and families were invited to these and soon formed new friendships. Retirement was turning out to be pretty good after all.

In 1980, a rather special invitation dropped through my letterbox. My wife and I were asked to attend an event called 'Rocket 150' celebrating 150 years of the Liverpool – Manchester Railway. It was to be held at Rainhill, Liverpool where, in 1840, locomotive trials were held that led to the opening of the railway.

The three-day celebrations were opened by the then Minister of Transport Norman Fowler, who arrived in a special train consisting of ex-LNER royal coaches pulled by LNW locomotive no. 790, named *HARDWICK*. The highlight of each day was to be a cavalcade of locomotives and rolling stock, all beautifully turned out and commemorating 150 years of railway history. For those wanting something more there were tented areas holding almost 200 trade displays and souvenir stands. Bands played and Morris Men danced and jingled, a funfair gave rides from morning until evening and little ones enjoyed the nursery playground. Over 120,000 people paid the £6 entrance fee to see the parade; millions more watched on television sets both in this country and many others.

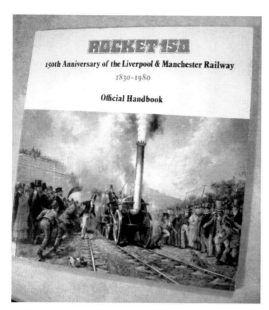

Souvenir programme of the Rocket 150 event in 1980.

We went to Rainhill on the third day. The weather was showery but didn't spoil our enjoyment. Forty locomotives were stabled in sidings at Bold Colliery, waiting to take their place in the cavalcade which passed slowly along the two-mile track between the colliery and Rainhill station and then back again. We took our place in the rows of seats which had been placed all along the railway embankment, affording a great view of this fascinating event. A wonderful replica of Stephenson's *ROCKET* led the parade, perfect in every respect except for its shortened chimney which had to be two feet lower so that it could pass under the bridges. We felt fortunate to see this because the engine had been derailed right at the start and missed the first day's proceedings. However, here it was with its open passenger wagon, the driver and fireman in their top hats and the ten passengers in period costume.

Another replica followed and this was the *SANS PAREIL*, a loco which had been built locally at Shildon works. *LION* was not a replica; no, at 142 years old this was the oldest locomotive in the world to be in full running order, and it was a privilege to see it. Many locos followed, taking us through the various stages of locomotion development until at last we came to the high speed trains and the Advanced Passenger Train of the 1980s. Truly, it was a day to remember.

I took up oil painting during the cold winter months and managed to surprise myself after a while by turning out one or two quite passable pictures. I live in Oxfordshire now but my painting of the waterfront at Liverpool hangs on the wall opposite my chair. The Merseyside area was in a deep depression when Kath and I decided to move nearer to our daughter. Big firms had left the area and the iron and steel trade was hitting rock bottom. On one of my walks I counted over 100 houses for sale. It seemed that lots of people were moving out but nobody wanted to move in. We'd decided to sell at a difficult time. But after 13 months we sold the house and moved into Eynsham in Oxfordshire.

A different kind of life; in Oxfordshire with the grandchildren in 1985.

Although we'd loved West Kirby we settled down well. I continued my walks around the new area and one day when I was strolling along, thinking about life in general, it struck me that I was the last remaining Barford in the family. The name would disappear when I'd gone. So I decided to do some research into my ancestry. It would have been much easier now with access to the internet, but back then I began very simply with birth certificates and gravestones. Lots of visits to Northamptonshire and eventually some help from a professional researcher took us back to December, 1600. This project had the added benefit of discovering relatives I didn't know I had, including some in New Zealand, so I felt very satisfied to have new family contacts and 400 years of history.

My walks eventually became cycle rides after a foot problem. The old single-speed bike became a 1948 three-speed Elswick Hopper, which in turn became a much lighter, modern one with 21 gears. This was followed by the nice new bike with the motor that I ride today. Over the years I've enjoyed riding around the countryside and I've clocked up nearly 37,000 miles so far.

It's a very different mode of transport from those great, steaming, smoking machines that fascinated me all my working life. Now, to try and find a conclusion to my tale of life on the railways is proving more difficult than I imagined. After so many years, it still seems not all that long ago that I was maintaining steam locomotives in icy weather, with snow inches deep and spanners freezing to the ground where I had dropped them. Or working in the heat of summer in the confined space of a warm tank or boiler, and emerging soaked with sweat and spitting out the black soot from the oil lamps.

High in my thoughts are all the friends I had to leave behind at the various depots and offices where my railway career had taken me. We still keep in touch through Christmas cards, but gradually they're reducing in number. One stands out to me. The chairman of the Chester Superannuants' Club, W.G.H. Riley (Bill), was an exceptional person and I admired him. He was very active, raising the membership to over 300; it must have been beneficial to his health because a few years ago I had a card from him along with a photograph of his 100th birthday celebrations.

It was a proud day for me when I started life on the railways. In those days, to be a railwayman was something of an achievement and in many cases, fathers, sons and even grandfathers worked at the same depot. Both the medical examinations and interviews were very thorough and carried out by really experienced officers. Everything about railway work is so different now – even the weather, which used to cause us such difficulties, seems to have changed. Although this past winter was the exception and took me back to the days of keeping all those fires burning!

I must say that, although not all the times were good ones, most of them were and I still enjoyed every minute of my railway service. If it were possible to have my time over again I would choose exactly the same career. Now I am over 90 years of age, I really truly hope that some younger people will, through what I have written down, be able to understand what the LMS and British railways were like in the years from 1932 to 1978.